P9-DGQ-073

NEVER

ALONE

~

ALSO BY JOSEPH F. GIRZONE

Joshua
Joshua and the Children
Joshua in the Holy Land
Kara, the Lonely Falcon
The Shepherd

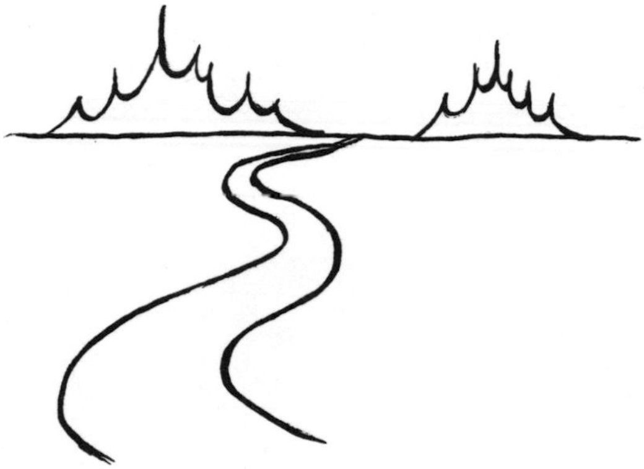

NEVER

ALONE

~

A Personal Way to God

JOSEPH F. GIRZONE

DOUBLEDAY

New York   London   Toronto   Sydney   Auckland

PUBLISHED BY DOUBLEDAY
a division of Bantam Doubleday Dell Publishing Group, Inc.
1540 Broadway, New York, New York 10036

DOUBLEDAY and the portrayal of an anchor with a dolphin are
trademarks of Doubleday, a division of Bantam Doubleday Dell
Publishing Group, Inc.

Book design by Claire Naylon Vaccaro

Library of Congress Cataloging-in-Publication Data

Girzone, Joseph F.
  Never alone : a personal way to God / Joseph F. Girzone.
  p.   cm.
  1. Spiritual life—Catholic Church.   2. Girzone, Joseph F.
3. Catholic Church—Membership.   I. Title.
BX2350.2.G57   1994
248.4'82—dc20   93-38725
                                                          CIP

ISBN 0-385-47342-7

Copyright © 1994 by Joseph F. Girzone
All Rights Reserved
Printed in the United States of America
March 1994
First Edition

1   3   5   7   9   10   8   6   4   2

Dedication

I dedicate this book to my friend who is always by my side and in my heart, who is never far when I am lonely and confused, who always gives peace to my soul when I am troubled and frightened, and fearful of the future. I share with Him my deepest secrets, my joy, my sorrow, my accomplishments, my shame. He always understands. He never accuses or criticizes, but often suggests a different way of doing things. When He does He inevitably prepares the way so it is not as impossible as I thought it might be. Over the years I have learned to trust Him. It was not easy. I thought that in following Him I would have to give up all the fun in my life, but I found that He is the Source of all joy and adventure, and, indeed, He turned my life into a great adventure at a time when I thought it was about to come to an end. I would like to suggest that He could become your Friend, too, if you would like Him to be. Do not be afraid! He will respect your freedom and your independence more than anyone you have ever met, because He created you to be free. He just wants more than anything that you will accept Him as your Friend. If you do, I can promise you, you will never be alone.

Acknowledgments

There are so many who have been part of the fabric of this book, I could never thank them all. I feel I do have to express my gratitude to at least a few who helped me in the preparation of the manuscript. Richard and Elizabeth Della Ratta, Sister Dorothy Ederer, O.P., and Lowell Rinker, my good friends, drawing on the richness of their own spiritual experiences, have helped greatly with their suggestions and support. Thomas Cahill and Trace Murphy at Doubleday have amazed me with their expert knowledge of the subject dealt with in the manuscript. Their advice and guidance have been invaluable. I am continually grateful to my good friend, Peter Ginsberg, who never loses faith in me. And then there is my loyal staff, Rosemary McGowan, Grace Falvo, Barbara Buffa, Joseph Bashant, David Bogatka, and Peter and Joseph Della Ratta, without whose help I would accomplish very little indeed. Finally, I just have to thank my friends at the Altamont Post Office for being so patient with me when I fly down there at the last minute with overnight deliveries to my publisher.

NEVER

ALONE

∾

I

ALONE

THE FIRST FRIEND I ever had lived next door. I was two years old. Not long after we first became friends, he moved. I lost my first friend and felt the first pain of loss. He was just a playmate; we merely shared each other's sandboxes, so it did not hurt much. Being very affectionate, however, I fell in love easily as a child. When I was four years old I fell madly in love with a beautiful girl named Thelma Stewart. I dreamed about her all day long and could not wait until three-thirty when school was out so I could stand at the street corner and watch her walk past with her friends. I don't think she even knew I existed. One day after school she was standing on the corner talking with her friends. Then she got on a bus, as her friends all said good-bye. I somehow knew I would never see her again. She never once looked at me or even acknowledged that she noticed me. My heart ached as the bus pulled away. My world crumbled, but I don't think I told anyone. I kept the suffering to myself, just as I would always keep it to myself. Pain seemed endless after that. Other friends came into my life, and just as casually left. It took me a long time to forget Thelma. My life as a child was terribly lonely. I was shy and could not talk to people I felt love for, so I wandered in a world of fantasy and dreams. I learned very young that I was alone in a world where everyone seemed a stranger, and that you could not hold on to even those you loved. They only too easily slipped away from you. And even more painful, there was no assurance that those I loved, loved me in return. People impressed me as being without feeling. They just laughed and talked, and said funny things that made others laugh, but had no real feeling for one another.

I used to think I was odd. As I grew older, though, and saw so much of others' pain, I began to realize that the whole world is filled with pain. I was not unique in feeling alone on a planet way out in the middle of space. Everyone eventually has the same experience in life. Friends come and go, passing in and out of your life. Strangers establish a friendship when they need you, then when their need is resolved, they drift. If you are sincere in your friendship this is hard to understand. People you love remain for a time, then they too leave when they outgrow their need for you. If at the twilight of your life you have one dear friend who has endured the fickleness of existence and remained in your life you are blessed. But, for the most part, you walk alone, very much alone.

I do not feel this experience of isolation was harmful in any way or had a negative effect on my life. I mention it only as a premise to where it led me psychologically and spiritually. I think it is more or less the lot of being human. All of us, no matter how extroverted we might be, are very much alone, not necessarily lonely, but alone, unable to share with anyone the deepest secrets of our hearts. I did not realize it then, but emotional and psychological pain was to become, perhaps, the most powerful force in molding the course of my life. For some people, pain and hurt breeds bitterness and cynicism. For others it causes them to look deeply into themselves and into life itself in an attempt to understand the meaning beneath seemingly capricious or arbitrary happenings.

I was fortunate as a child to have been introduced to God. My mother said my prayers with me each night, and developed in me a sense of Jesus as a person who cared for me. This took hold. I don't know what path my life would have taken if I had had different experiences during that sensitive time in my life. But having found that God could be a real friend, I could share my secrets with Him. When I made my First Communion, I was filled with the comforting realization that Jesus was now an intimate part of my life. On my own I went to Mass every morning so I could receive Communion and spend time in church by myself just sitting and thinking of God. He was real to me, not make-believe, but a living presence. I sensed His presence in a way that made me feel as if my soul was floating inside me. It was more than emotion. It was more than just a need for a friend to fill the emptiness of a child's loneliness. His presence touched my being and I knew He was with me, and it affected my life profoundly. When I was hurting, I would talk to Jesus about it, or tell His mother. I sensed Jesus heard me and even though He might not do anything tangible in response, I knew He heard me and I knew He was nearby to give me strength. Jesus did say after all that for those who accept Him, He and His Father would come and live within them.

I think, perhaps, that finding God at such a young age may not have been a common experience, but I am grateful that it happened to me. My awareness and understanding of Jesus had a much longer period of time to expand and mature. I had a chance to evaluate and relate events and life's experiences to my relationship with Him during my childhood, my adolescence, and my whole adult life. During my years of theological studies I could filter what I learned in theology through my experiences with Jesus. This made it possible for me to take the cold, finely chiseled theological concepts and transform them into a living expression of the way Jesus thought and envisioned life. Though theology was cold and sterile in its intellectual expression, it was for me a vehicle for understanding the mind of God and for developing a precise sense of God, and a healthy realization that God could not be defined or limited by human concepts. I also saw from our extensive study of Scriptures that God had a sense of morality that was much more open than the narrow, rigid morality of moral theologians, or even the Church itself. That was to affect radically my understanding of people later on when they came to me with very disturbing moral problems. I could always see abundant goodness alongside the very severe moral weakness in people, and learned to treat them as whole persons and not as sinners, the way Jesus, for example, treated the Samaritan woman who was married five times and did not even bother to marry the last person. Jesus still saw goodness in her and decided one day to meet with her and chose her to announce the Good News to that Samaritan village. Churches do not treat people that way. Sinners are very carefully avoided in our churches and are not allowed to take part in the real life of the church. We do not feel comfortable with sinners and we make them feel uncomfortable by not allowing them to perform services and ministries that are open to others whose lives superficially are more in keeping with Church standards. Jesus, on the other hand, was open to people who had glaring defects, and saw them in the wholeness of their lives, and saw in their lives the goodness that far outshone their weaknesses. He could pick a publican, Levi, with the bad reputation publicans had, to be not just a disciple but an apostle. He Himself got a reputation for going to the homes of excommunicated people for parties, because as the Good Shepherd He continually reached out to the bruised and hurting sheep. We, on the contrary, tell the bruised and hurting sheep they cannot approach Jesus because they are not worthy.

That is why a precise understanding of Jesus is so important for us, so we can share His vision of God and His understanding of human nature and frame for ourselves our own relationship with God within the context of the rest of His creation. If Christianity is merely a theological system, it will at most produce a highly educated elite devoid of anything resembling the living

Christ in their personal lives. We saw this recently in the presidential campaign, when one of the candidates, well educated theologically, was spewing forth the most shockingly un-Christ-like invectives and ridicule against homosexuals and homeless people, showing a lack of sensitivity and compassion that betrayed a poverty of spirituality that shocked most decent people.

Unfortunately, so much energy in ecclesiastical institutions is used in validating theological and social positions in relation to other denominations and the secular world that the fundamental purpose of religion, to foster and mold spirituality among its members, fades out of focus. Thus, we are faced with the masses of Christians wandering the globe trying to find their own way to God, while religious professionals and religious news publishers engage in the much more ego-rewarding task of fighting global issues. The consciences of religious leaders and religious media people can be sensitive to the physical starvation of people around the world, for which they are to be commended, but they seem so often to be totally insensitive to the much more devastating spiritual starvation of people in their neighborhood, for whom they are immediately responsible. Rarely do you hear clergy talk about spirituality, or teach their people the ways of prayer and how to develop a deeper intimacy with God. Perhaps, they don't know how. Perhaps that has never been a priority with many clergy. We teach theology, we explain Scriptures, we enact nice liturgies, we debate public issues, we parade the streets in protest marches. That is good form and intellectually challenging. The world of the spirit, however, is the substance of religion and the pilgrim's path through that world is devoid of expert guides. For this frightfully labyrinthian journey, fraught with so many pitfalls and mine fields, we as clergy rarely provide people with the tools they need to find their way to God.

This struck me very clearly when I was in a country where Buddhism was popular. Relaxing in my hotel room one day, I picked up a copy of a book on Buddha. After giving a synopsis of Buddha's life, the book went on to describe his way of life and principles for healthy spiritual living. The rest of the book contained a detailed description of how Buddha arrived at his vision of life and how his followers, in imitating him, could find their way to inner peace. We don't do that with Jesus. We have endless books about whether He existed, or whether the Jesus we have learned about is really accurate and historical or mythical. We have endless complicated tracts on fine technical issues, but we don't explore Jesus' way to happiness and peace, or try to understand His feelings about God and creation or how He views our relationship with God, or His attitude toward human weakness. Understanding these things could help us immensely in our own search for inner peace and a meaning to life. Indeed, it is a rare seminary today that teaches anything about Jesus other than in Christology courses, which in several prestigious seminaries I know of are merely offered as electives.

I have learned so many things about people's spiritual needs since the Joshua books became popular. Having heard so frequently that people's interest in religion had fallen off dramatically, I was shocked at the almost universal response of the public to *Joshua*. It was not just Catholics and Episcopalians, and Lutherans and Presbyterians, but Baptists, Pentecostals, Evangelicals, Jews, Moslems, Hindus, Buddhists, Sikhs, and not just adults, but children down to nine years old. Catholic priests wrote letters of thanks, saying Joshua saved their priesthood. Baptist ministers told me after talks, with tears in their eyes, that Joshua healed them of burdens they had carried all their lives, and brought them to a new and beautiful understanding of Jesus. Jews wrote and told me they read *Joshua* and have developed a beautiful relationship with Jesus, and want to follow His way of life privately. The same with people of other religions, and even those with no religion. What all this said to me in a powerful way was that people may be tired of religion, but they are desperately hungering for a relationship with God that can empower them with a new vision of life and heal wounds that have been festering for a lifetime, and renew their zest for living.

People's searching for spirituality is almost epidemic. For the past twenty years or more, Westerners have traveled to the Far East searching for happiness in Eastern religions. Conversely, Hindus and Buddhists from the East are searching for a meaning to life here in the West. A group of Hindus contacted me after reading *Joshua,* asking me if I would be their guru. They told me they found such peace in *Joshua* they wanted to learn more about Jesus' way of life. They asked if I would guide them in their search for peace and happiness and a deeper relationship with God. This search for a meaning to life and an intimacy with God is not limited to Westerners, it is universal. And that is precisely the reason Jesus came to earth, to teach us the way. "I am the way, the truth and the life," He said. That is what we have lost sight of, Christianity as the way. What is so troubling about our religion today is that the clergy either don't recognize the people's hunger for spirituality or are unfamiliar themselves with Jesus' way of life and Christianity's rich tradition of mysticism and asceticism, all well tested through the centuries. This is Christianity and application of Jesus' teachings at its best, and we don't teach it to our people. At the height of the Protestant Reformation, St. Teresa of Avila and St. John of the Cross, St. Ignatius Loyola, and others were delineating the path of interior holiness through mystical union with God in such practical detail that even today their approach to holiness is still taught in theology courses and spiritual retreats. Sadly, the masses of the people are not taught this in their churches, so not even knowing that such guidance exists, they look outside Christianity.

Parents may teach religion to children. Churches may do the same. But that is not spirituality. That, too, should begin in childhood. Children should be taught about God in a simple, loving way so they can learn to trust Him and begin to know Him as a kind and loving Father who made them, not perfectly but with all they need to grow in His love. They could be taught about Jesus and about His life and how He lived and how He loved people. They could be taught about Jesus as the Good Shepherd who cared for the hurting and the troubled sheep, so they can learn to run to Him when they have problems, and when they fall and make mistakes.

Ordinarily, spirituality is not a child's venture. Spiritual growth like growth in any other facet of our lives is a process. It works through phases. The spiritual life is most frequently activated after some personal crisis or tragedy. To force a strong spirituality on children before they are ready is unnatural and can kill a child's interest in religion and even in God. We can introduce a child to God and plant the seed that will in God's good time germinate and grow, but moving in a world of spiritual things is not really what interests young people. In fact it can be harmful to demand too much from them when they are too young to even understand the meaning of the word "spirituality." So many of my friends in their excessive zeal to arouse their children's spiritual lives saturated them with religious activities. When the children became adolescents, they couldn't stand religion and went to church only after horrendous fights. The older children stopped going to church altogether.

Eventually people come to a realization of their need for God, and their need to grow spiritually. Real spirituality and spiritual growth, however, has to be distinguished from religious activities and pious exercises. These exercises merely mimic spirituality. Unfortunately, many people think that they grow close to God by performing religious practices and doing religious things. That is not spirituality. They may even get a reputation for being pious. Jesus lived for thirty years in Nazareth, and you would think the townsfolk He grew up with would have been impressed with His holiness. Oddly enough, they were surprised when He began His public mission and began to preach the Good News. "Where did he get all this from? Isn't this the carpenter's son?" Obviously, His holiness didn't make a big impression. You might wonder how Jesus could have kept His exquisite spirituality hidden during all those years, so that even His playmates were shocked by His apparent newfound interest in religion. What made it possible for Jesus to keep His spiritual life hidden from the eyes of those who lived so close to Him was that His holiness was genuine. It did not depend on showy external practices. "When you pray, go to your room and lock your door," He advised the apostles, "and pray to your Father in secret and your Father who knows what is secret will hear you." And on another occasion, He remarked to His disciples that they should not be like the scribes and Pharisees who love to recite long prayers and be seen praying in public. "Do not do your good deeds to be seen by others. Those who do such things already have their reward."

Remarks like this give a good indication of where Jesus was coming from and the attitudes that guided His own life-style.

The mistake many people make when they start trying to be holy is they multiply religious practices and burden themselves with a host of activities, attending endless religious services, thinking that the more good things they do, the more spiritual they become. Spirituality doesn't work that way. The spiritual life is something that grows slowly, imperceptibly, way beneath the surface of our lives. Pressuring ourselves to do all kinds of nice things for people and performing a multitude of good works does not make us holy. It can, if we are not careful, make us extremely nervous and pressure us into commitments that can overload our already overburdened lives.

Real spirituality begins by finding God, feebly, perhaps, in the beginning, but then more confidently as we travel along the way. At first, we may be driven to Him out of desperation. But that's all right. God uses all kinds of circumstances to lead us to Himself. Or we may just feel a need to draw closer to God. Whatever the reason, God is calling us to a deeper intimacy with Himself. Jesus teaches us the attitudes we should have when we establish contact with His Father. We must have a childlike trust. This isn't a command, but His attempt to teach us how to establish a healthy relationship with His Father whom He knows so well. "Why are you all so worried?" He said to the crowd one day. "Look at the birds of the air. They don't sow and they don't reap and they don't gather into barns. Your heavenly Father takes care of them. You are worth more than all the flocks of birds and all you do is worry, as if you never had a heavenly Father. Stop worrying. Your heavenly Father knows what you need, even before you ask Him."

That is the beginning of spirituality, recognizing the need for God in our lives, and placing ourselves in His hands with complete trust, confident of the tenderness of our Father's love for us. We may have a difficulty with this, because all of us are only too conscious of our many failings and feel we do not have a right to God's kindness toward us. But that is precisely what makes God's love so beautiful. It does not spring from the goodness He sees in us, but from the overflowing good-ness of His own love and the compassion He has for us in our weakness and sinfulness. The crowd Jesus ad-dressed on that occasion when He spoke of the birds of the air were just ordinary people, sinners like ourselves, if you want to call them that, although Jesus didn't call them sinners. Jesus called people God's children and "little flock." It is touching the tender way Jesus spoke to the crowd that day assuring them of His Father's concern, even though He was only too aware of the serious moral defects in their lives. So, when we begin our adventure with God, it is with the assurance that He is open to us and kindly disposed toward us. We do not approach Him as a nuisance. In spite of our past lives and frightful weaknesses, He is glad we are turning to Him. Like the prodigal father of the prodigal son, He greets us with open arms, and is only too ready to share with us His friendship and His boundless mercy. All is forgiven, all is renewed. Though our sins be as scarlet, He will cleanse us and make us white as snow, through a baptism if necessary, or through a reawakening of the baptismal life we have already received, and a healing reconciliation.

II

NOTHING/
EVERYTHING

ONE DAY JESUS made the remark, "The birds of the air have their nests, the foxes have their dens, but the son of man has nowhere to lay his head." I have thought about that so many times. On the surface it appeared as if Jesus was feeling sorry for Himself, but that mentality was so far removed from His way of thinking that it didn't even make sense. What Jesus seemed to be saying was "Look at me, I have nothing, not even a place to sleep, and I am perfectly happy." The common purse He oddly enough turned over to Judas, even though He knew he could not be trusted to handle money, showed how little value Jesus attached to material things. This attitude of Jesus toward material things is basic to an understanding of His spirituality. He had one robe, no second change of clothes, no purse. He slept very frequently up in the hills where the Gospel writers say He would spend the night in prayer. He and His followers apparently depended to a great extent on the generosity of people along the way to care for their material needs, especially for food. "Do not worry about what you will eat or what you will drink" was an admonition He practiced in His own life. Yet, He showed no objection to those of His followers who were well-to-do. Mary, Martha, and Lazarus were by no means poor. Zacchaeus, the chief tax collector, was a very wealthy man. Joseph of Arimathea was also a wealthy follower of Jesus. Even the rich young man who approached Jesus one day asking Him what he must do to be saved. All Jesus told Him was "Keep the commandments." Only when the man expressed dissatisfaction with that answer, did Jesus tell him, "If you want to be perfect, go sell what you have and give to the poor." But Jesus did not demand it. He suggested it because the man indicated he wanted to do something more than just the minimum.

Jesus Himself was "poor," by choice. He was born "poor." He had a manger for a crib. He had the wherewithal to be "rich." He chose not to be. His poverty was logical for Him. He knew who He was. Material things could add nothing to His image of Himself. They were to Him just like the dirt in the field; gold merely a type of stone, clothes something made from animal skins or culled from plants that grew in the fields. He needed no material things to enhance His self-image or His reputation in other people's eyes. What He had to offer was infinitely more valuable. Freedom of spirit and the joy that flows from that freedom were essential to Jesus. It was this spirit He tried to pass on to those who would follow Him. "Blessed are the poor in spirit, theirs is the kingdom of heaven." He did not say blessed are those in material or financial need, but the poor in spirit. Theirs is the freedom and the joy and the peace of the children of God, the kingdom of heaven. This was the condition for finding the joy that Jesus possessed and which He wanted His followers to experience. It was fundamental to Jesus' approach to spirituality. Place your trust in your heavenly Father who knows what you need, and do not worry yourself about the things of this world. He will give you what you need.

When I was young, my father, who was a butcher, used to take me and my brothers and sisters to help him in his store. He had a good business with mostly well-to-do customers—judges, lawyers, doctors, government officials, businesspeople. He was a good butcher and would go to the packing houses to pick the cuts of meat his customers preferred. Often there were customers waiting for him outside his store when he arrived in the morning, because they knew they would have the best selection of cuts early in the day.

But despite his successful business, he never seemed concerned about material things. In the wintertime, my father wore an old overcoat with the pocket torn out. It never bothered him though my mother was forever trying to fix it. Also, he could not wear overshoes because they hurt his feet. He had ulcerated varicose veins that were painful. When there was snow on the ground he would wrap burlap around his shoes. It looked so unfashionable to say the least. I was ashamed, I couldn't even get out of the truck with him. Four or five people were waiting for him to open the store. When my father got out of the truck, an immaculately dressed judge who was a good friend commented, "That's quite an outfit you've got there, Peter!" My father smiled and replied good-naturedly, "Yes, Judge, you have to have dignity."

I asked my father one day why he dressed like that. He merely answered, "It is not what you wear that is important. It is what you are inside. Real dignity is in the beauty of your soul." I couldn't understand this way back then.

When I had to retire a number of years ago because of my health, I chose not to accept any compensation from the diocese, though I had no income. For the first time in my life I was nearly penniless. I had just enough to survive. I ate food many poor people would turn down. I had no money for clothes. I made my furniture from some boards I bought cheap. I had one plate, a bowl, a couple of glasses, and three utensils. I knew for the first time in my life what it was to be genuinely "poor," in the world's sense of the word. But these were the happiest days of my life, even though I had nothing. I had to practice what Jesus taught and what I had preached all my life, "Look at the birds of the air . . ." and I learned from experience what my dad tried to teach me, and what Jesus taught so beautifully in His own life. I learned it didn't take much to survive, not to live luxuriously, but to survive. But even with just the bare necessities, I had everything I needed to be happy.

One morning, I was taking a walk, and wondering what I would do for supper, since I had no money. Walking along the side of the road I thought I saw some money in the ditch. But how would money get into that ditch so far from anyplace? I took a closer look and bent down and sure enough, there, lying in the ditch and neatly folded, was some money, just enough for supper.

I could almost hear Jesus saying, "I told you not to worry, I would take care of you." Jesus was right and I could now say that from my own firsthand experience.

A short time later, that all changed. When *Joshua* became popular, money became a painful burden. Trying to use it wisely was not easy.

Jesus' attitude seems to be that freedom from material possessions can be very liberating. Having money and being free is also possible but adds complicated responsibilities which can jeopardize that freedom. The important thing is to maintain a detachment from whatever possessions we may have, whether they be great or small, and not allow ourselves to become so concerned about them that they become a serious distraction from our own inner growth. "Where your heart is there your treasure lies." However, a person does not have to have great wealth to be attached. A poor person can be even more obsessed with his few possessions than a rich person with his vast wealth.

The freedom and peace Jesus talked about had to do not only with material things but with anything that generated undue anxiety which could disturb our inner well-being. One of the most remarkable things about Jesus' life is His tranquillity. When you consider the almost constant turmoil that surrounded Jesus—crowds pressing in on Him, and His enemies plotting daily to destroy Him—and see the calmness that pervaded His life, it is remarkable, and proves the value of the detachment that Jesus had from whatever could disturb his inner peace. That detachment Jesus tried to share with his followers so they, too, could find the same power and inner peace that marked His life.

If there was one thing Jesus held out to his followers it was His promise of peace. "Peace I leave with you, my peace I give you." He never tired of speaking about the peace that He would give to those who accepted His way of life. This theme threads its way through the whole Gospel message. It is a trademark of His spirituality, and should be a trait that singles out His disciples, in whatever age they live.

Why, then, we might wonder, do Jesus' followers not stand out for their peacefulness? The answer is simple. His disciples through all time are not familiar with the message as Jesus delivered it. We are brought up to follow unquestioningly the practices of our religion, whatever our denomination. But obedience to customs and dictates of religion does not make a follower of Jesus. Though many talk about accepting the Lord Jesus and about commitment to Him, frequently that acceptance has little to do with Jesus Himself. It is acceptance of the teacher who has delivered the message and the way of life laid out by the teacher that people follow. It is not the message of Jesus that is being followed, but the guidance and interpretation of the teacher. He or she becomes the way of life. This is not an immediate personal relationship with Jesus.

The one thing that is absolutely necessary if we are to develop a spirituality based on Jesus' life is that we open our hearts to the Person of Jesus Himself, and allow Him to come into our lives to befriend us and guide us. He promised, "I will not leave you orphans; I will come to you . . . He who loves me will be loved by my Father, and I will love him and manifest myself to him." This is the essence of Christian spirituality, the living presence of Jesus in our souls. He is there, not as a dummy, neither hearing nor speaking, but as an active partner in our lives, guiding and comforting us when we need Him. It is this mystical friendship with Jesus that is the core of Christian spirituality, and makes Christian spirituality a unique custom-designed journey fashioned after the uniqueness of each individual person.

Once we open ourselves to God, and show a willingness to follow His grace in our lives, we want to see immediate results. But we are really traveling in a foreign land. Spirituality is a real journey into the unknown. What are the parameters, the rules, the pathways? Where do they lead? Does everyone follow the same road, and become like everyone else on this unusual journey? Do you give up your personality and suppress your real self so you can become a new person?

Many people feel they have to shed their old selves when they enter the spiritual life, and become saintly overnight. It doesn't work that way. We don't grow physically overnight. Neither do we grow emotionally or mentally overnight. Growth consists of long involved processes. It is the same with the spiritual life. We grow gradually, over a lifetime. Just like physical growth cannot be forced, so spiritual growth cannot be forced without doing severe damage, because we then pressure ourselves to do things perfectly before we have developed the underlying strength and charity from which perfection spontaneously flows. Each one grows the way God planned for us to grow, depending upon what He had in mind for each of us. Grace builds upon nature, as St. Paul writes. It does not destroy nature.

What is it, then, that God has in mind? Perhaps we will never know. Nor is it important that we know. What is important is that we leave ourselves open to God each day so He can use us as He sees fit. That's His business. We are merely His creatures, His servants. To be at His disposal is our responsibility. Humility has to be a fundamental condition of our relationship with God. But we can be sure that He will use us and His using us will always be exciting and always an adventure. Many people are afraid of giving themselves to God, and letting God into their lives, because they think all their fun will come to an end and life will become a bore. There is one thing God is not, though, and that is boring. The creative imagination of God is beyond comprehension, and the real fun in our lives just begins once we find God and He becomes an active partner in our lives. My own life became a whirlwind when I made up my mind that I was not going to forge my own way through life but instead would let God guide me. And it makes good sense. God didn't create us haphazardly. He made each of us for a purpose and He is determined that we accomplish that purpose. He does, however, need our cooperation, and when we give Him our goodwill and open our hearts to Him (which is really all we have to offer), He sets in motion all the machinery we need to fulfill the task He has planned for us. That is always exciting and rewarding, because the gifts and talents He has given us are perfectly adapted to the work He has designed for us. That is the perfect blueprint for success, happiness, and fulfillment.

III

A FRIEND

FOREVER

THE RELATIONSHIP WITH Jesus we discussed in the last chapter, like any relationship, has to be cultivated. Relationship with Christ is cultivated through prayer. I know when I mention the word "prayer," many people will immediately be turned off. Prayer does not have a happy connotation in many people's minds. It is for them a boring, futile exercise, talking to someone who never talks back, sharing with someone who never responds, pleading when you're desperate and not getting any answers, like talking to a wall. That is not the kind of prayer I am talking about. People get frustrated with prayer because they are looking for an instant response and when it doesn't happen, they get discouraged. It is as if God should be like a genie, rub the lamp and get immediate action. God does not work that way. He is not a God of quick fixes. He is a very patient God who heals gently and thoroughly.

The kind of prayer I am talking about is a detached kind of prayer in which you are not looking for anything, just putting yourself in God's presence and sharing with Him what you are feeling or what you are suffering. It is the kind of prayer in which you just open your heart to God and say, "God, I'm here. I'm not asking for anything, God. I just want to be near you and open my heart to you. I need you, Lord, and I'm here at your disposal. Whatever you want to do with me, Lord, I'm ready. I don't know what to say to you. I don't know what to ask you. I don't even understand what is important for me. You know it all beforehand anyway. I know you have much to share with me, Lord, and I am finally ready to listen. Speak to me, Lord, my heart is open to you. But, Lord, please don't leave me alone."

This kind of prayer is most effective. It is not demanding of an immediate response. God doesn't work that way anyway. It is a prayer that comes from a humble heart, the kind that God can work with because a humble heart is ready to listen. It leaves God the leeway to subtly work within us, gently touching our thoughts and our feelings, quietly adjusting our vision, so that when we look at things in His creation around us, we see precious gifts to be treasured and not just things to be used, or abused, and discarded. When we look at people, even obnoxious people, we see Him in them and treat Him accordingly. When we are hurting, we know He is there, and we know He will turn our pain into a grace. We don't even have to ask Him. This openness in our prayer life becomes a permanent condition of childlike trust which places us in a continuous state of readiness when He speaks to us, in whatever way He chooses to communicate.

The detachment which is an essential element in this kind of prayer is what places us at God's disposal. It renders us supple, and malleable and workable in God's hands. It makes us usable, which is what God desperately wants from all of us but what He rarely receives from any of us. It gives our uniqueness the chance to be utilized to our maximum potential, the uniqueness for which God created us originally, to accomplish something special with our lives.

This detachment is difficult, so we may have to work at it. It includes detachment not only from material things, but a detachment from our own inner needs which pressure us constantly to carry out our own agenda, no matter what God may want, because we can't afford to allow our needs to go unattended. It is our inability to let go of our fancied or contrived needs that makes detachment so difficult and throws us into endless fits of depression. Even though we may have to struggle to arrive at a workable level of detachment, it is well worth it, because it is the key to opening our soul to God's grace and our own ensuing peace.

When I was in theology studies (I was about twenty-four at the time), I reached a point in my spiritual life that for me was critical. I would have liked to have worked in Rome, maybe in the Vatican doing diplomatic work. I really didn't have much hope of it, but if I wanted to be political enough I could have worked my way wherever I wanted to be. I had at the time written a paper for mystical theology class. The professor called me down to his room and asked me to explain the paper to him, telling me he had read the paper a number of times but it was so deep he had a difficult time understanding it. When I explained it to him, he was impressed and asked if I would like to work in Rome. He told me I had a rare speculative mind, and there was a great need for speculative theologians. I told him I would like that and he said he would see what he could do. Nothing ever came of it, and I decided I would do nothing to remind him, even after he became the superior general in Rome. I had reached the point in my spiritual life where I had decided that I would place myself completely in God's hands and never scheme for the things I wanted.

That decision in a way was devastating, because the assignments I was given after that were very difficult for me. I was sent to teach at one of my order's high schools in the Bronx, and was shocked when there was no priest in the house to welcome me. A priest visiting from Holland told me after two hours of waiting to be assigned a room that all the priests had left as their way of telling me they didn't want me there. It being my first assignment I was devastated, but decided that this was God's problem, not mine. Though no one talked to me for weeks, I did my work and steeled myself against the callous behavior of these grown men, religious men. I was eventually told there were problems in the school, many of the kids were on parole, and they had asked the provincial superior for a strong, muscular priest who weight-lifted, and when they got me instead, a skinny hundred-forty-pound shadow, they resented it, until I became popular with the students as well as the faculty. Then things changed.

A few years later I was sent out to a mining area in Pennsylvania. After the four years of high activity and social life in New York City, the change was difficult. My stay in Pennsylvania eventually became one of the happiest of my life, even though I went through much heartache. After that I was sent to teach in the seminary, then in other places without any apparent logic. My assignments after that were varied and I found myself assigned to work for which I had no training or preparation, working among Jews, among Protestants of various denominations, among elderly, in tumultuous community situations, with prison riots, and consequent reform efforts, with review boards monitoring conditions in youth prisons, and a host of problems I had never faced before. And the strange paradox was that all I really wanted to do was study and write.

Fortunately, I never rebelled against all these apparently unexplainable assignments, because all these varied situations ultimately provided me with the experiences I needed to be able to write the way I do, and place Joshua in so many varied circumstances that give depth and credibility to the Joshua stories. Without those experiences my writings would have been impossible. As it is, Joshua has affected the lives of literally millions of people all over the world. So, from personal experience, I can see in a powerful way the value of detaching ourselves from our personal needs and ambitions and placing ourselves in God's hands so He can guide us. It works.

Some might object that this approach detracts from the self-reliance we should have, and places us at the mercy of uncontrollable forces in our lives. That might be true if there were no God who cares. That would be blind abandonment to irrational forces. Our whole approach to spirituality, however, is based on the premise that there is a God, and that He is a God who cares. Now that I am older I can see the orderly way God works in people's lives. Our early years, while they may seem rife with turmoil and pain and so many loose ends, when viewed from the distance of later life and our personal development, we can see as being the foundation and the training process for the rewarding work God has planned for our future. I don't mean the job we may have for our subsistence. I mean the thrust of our personal life with all its encounters and relationships and the various ways we affect people as well as the influence we have on the world around us in our family and in our social as well as our business life.

Take the life of Moses, for example. Moses was an Israelite, born in Egypt. Pharaoh issued a decree that all Israelite boys under two years old were to be destroyed. Moses' mother hid the baby Moses in the rushes near Pharaoh's palace. Pharaoh's daughter found him and brought him into the palace, where he was raised as a member of the king's family. Later on he was given assignments in the Egyptian government and trained in administration. One day Moses saw an Egyptian soldier beating an Israelite slave, and he struck the soldier, accidentally killing him. There was a warrant put out for his arrest. From that point on his whole life changed.

Moses fled out into the Sinai desert where he wandered for years, and finally met the daughter of a nomad tribesman and married her. Later on God called Moses to go back to Egypt and to lead His people to freedom. For the next forty years Moses was occupied with the whole Hebrew nation, over half a million people, as they roamed aimlessly under God's guidance until they reached the promised land. You cannot help but feel that Moses' whole past life was a carefully planned preparation as God molded him for the great work He had in store for him. Without all the training Moses had in administration in Pharaoh's government, without the years of loneliness and soul-searching in his wanderings through the barren Sinai, Moses would have been ill-prepared for the giant task that lay ahead. Perhaps, even the tragic accident of killing the Egyptian soldier may have been part of the preparation in becoming the great lawgiver of civilization. Moses had to promulgate God's law with deep humility, knowing he broke one of the greatest of those commandments by destroying a human life.

You see the same thing in the lives of so many people who have had profound influence on others' lives. What made them great was not an accident. It was the years of painful preparation and training as God steeled their souls for the future. They were scorched and burned and tried by fire and pain as God worked secretly in the depths of their souls sharpening their vision of life and focusing their wisdom and understanding for the work they were to do.

The astonishing thing about this training process is that it is entirely different for each individual. St. Paul talked about the various gifts and functions in the mystical body of Christ. The Spirit works in different ways in different individuals as each one has his and her special function to perform in the building up of the mystical body. To do this special work each of us has to be specially prepared by God. Grace builds on nature, as God works in an orderly way in our lives, pouring grace upon grace as He molds our lives. Because of this no two people are alike, nor is spirituality a monolith where everyone is squeezed into the same mold. Each person's spiritual life is special and unique. Each of us is growing in our own way as God works miracles of grace deep within us, far from the prying eyes of the curious.

That is why it is so offensive when we pressure others to adopt our way of doing things and to change their ways so they will conform to our life-style or adopt our religious values. And I don't mean matters of vital importance like accepting God into our lives, but pressuring people to pray the way we pray or to exercise the gifts of the Spirit which we think they should have. That interferes with God's work in people's souls. It is obnoxious to pressure others in spiritual matters, for everyone is in a different stage along the way of spiritual growth. God Himself works with such sensitivity in each of our lives that for us to blunder into another person's intimacy with God is crude. Besides, we never really know what is going on in another's soul. We may make the judgment they are not holy and need us to prod them, but we can never know. True spirituality is so deep that a person could be a saint and it could be

hidden from people's eyes. We got where we are because God guided us, often after many years of not
responding we finally accepted His grace. Why should
we dare to interfere in another person's life and think
we can force them into a spiritual life overnight by pressuring them to death? That is not the way God's grace
works and the conversion may not even be genuine,
because it is the result of coercion or intimidation.

Each person's relationship with God is a mystery, a
mystery so deep we could never begin to fathom it. All
we know for sure is that God is fashioning a masterpiece of unimaginable beauty way beneath what the human eye can see or the human mind can comprehend.
Only in time as the plan begins to take shape will hints
of what is taking place beneath the surface begin to
emerge. I am sure each of us can see a pattern in the way
He has been working in our lives, more so if we are
older and have a better chance to view things from a
distance. We can see the good coming out of the difficult and sometimes devastating experiences of our
youth. I know I can. I went through a period of over ten
years of the most intense depression in my older teen
years until after my ordination. During that time I found
it so difficult to feel there was a God. Not that I did not
believe. My faith grew stronger than ever, but the darkness was almost impossible to bear, particularly since I
had had such a warm relationship with God up until
that point. Now I had to cling to God on sheer faith and
in darkness and pain, even on the day of my ordination.
Yet, those years were the most fruitful and productive

years of my life spiritually, as God helped me to grow in a deeper understanding of Himself and others, as well as myself. I do not think I would be capable of doing the work I do now if I had not gone through those experiences earlier in my life. What I learned then prepared me well for the future, although I doubt I would have the strength to endure that pain at this point in my life.

I do not think everyone would have to follow that route to God, but for me it was a necessity and it was effective. Others have radically different experiences depending upon how God is molding them and where He is leading them. The important lesson is that each of us is unique and special and we must allow God the freedom to work in our souls in whatever way He pleases, knowing that He is an accomplished Master and will produce in us a masterpiece.

IV

GOD, WHERE ARE YOU?

NOW THAT GOD has begun a work in us and we are learning to feel comfortable with His presence, we have to let go of fear and trust Him completely. This is most difficult. The apostles themselves found this difficult. Even after living with Jesus for years and seeing the wonders He could perform, they still could hesitate and doubt, in His very presence, like the time Jesus called Peter to come to Him across the stormy sea. Peter obeyed and walked on the water, then panicked when he realized what he was doing. We are so used to being in control. We are brought up to be independent, self-reliant; "to be responsible" we call it. It is not easy to abandon that control and let God into our lives, much less submit to His control. But it is the only way we can function successfully, and indeed survive. It is even more difficult for parents to turn over to God control of their children's lives. Parents often feel the only way they can protect their children is to control and direct their every move. When a child's life gets completely out of control, an overly protective parent can fall apart. They are so afraid their child is on the road to destruction. Yet, to turn the child over to God is the only way to really help the child, who may after all be twenty-five, thirty, or many years older. God is real and He is waiting for a chance to help if only we can ease up and give Him some space. It is not abandoning responsibility. It is not giving up. It is just an honest admission that we are incapable of handling life with all its frightening complications, some stemming from our own human frailty, others from outside ourselves. It is a plea for God to help us.

There is a solid theological basis for this abandonment to God founded on the fact that God did not create us haphazardly. He created each one of us with tender love and care and planned wonderful things for our lives, not just for ourselves but for those whose lives we will touch. He is concerned that we play our part in the world and influence others' lives while we grow within. Jesus once made the remark that His Father knows us so intimately He even knows the number of hairs on our head. This involvement by God is not to find fault, or to convict us, but to help us understand ourselves and to feel comfortable with His presence, and follow His guidance.

The more practical and independent we are the more difficult it is to be reliant on God. We are so used to analyzing situations and working out solutions to problems that to abandon ourselves to God and be open to His grace seems almost like a cop-out and shirking responsibility. Many people find it near impossible to understand. Yet, it is necessary if we are to develop a partnership with God, and that is what spirituality essentially is. We can do nothing without God because He has the key to the complex mystery of our lives, but He also needs us to fulfill His own plans for the development of His creation, which by His inten-tion is imperfect and incomplete. It is our function to help perfect His creation. He will not, however, violate our free will and force us to work with Him, even though He needs our cooperation to accomplish His goals in the world.

You see this in a global way. Whole nations are dying of starvation, while others have a glut of food. People become angry with God. "If God is good, how can He tolerate such evil and misery," they complain. It is not God's fault. God works with His human crea-tures. He works with them and through them. God always does His part. He gives us more than we need so we can share with others in need. We are the ones who disconnect from Him and refuse to carry our share of the burden, so we see anguish and pain everywhere.

It is the same in our personal lives. God wants to be part of our lives. We want to enjoy our independence, which we are afraid we will lose if we give God a foot-hold. We struggle and give up our stubbornness reluc-tantly. The strange thing is that all God wants for each of us is our happiness, and for us to enjoy the life He gives us. His purpose in wanting to become a partner is not to make our lives miserable, limit our joy, or restrict our freedom, but to gently point out for us how we can best accomplish our work and find peace and satisfac-tion in the process. That is all God wants from us. To aid in this, Jesus promised that when we accept Him, He and His Father come and live within us.

I do not think people realize what a stupendous privilege this is. We read those words in the Gospel and it does not strike us as sensational. However, to think that Jesus is promising to establish a personal relationship with us and to be with us, not just by our side but within us, as a friend and companion, that is so comforting and so assuring. From then on we will never be alone.

Abandoning ourselves to God does not mean we stop thinking or dreaming about life or our future. Our life really does not change. We still get up in the morning, say our prayers, plan our schedule, go about doing what we would normally do. The only thing that changes is that we are now open for God to involve Himself in our lives, and when circumstances point very clearly that God is saying something to us, we listen and, no matter how busy we may be, we follow where He leads. That will happen more and more often once we have found Him. He arranges circumstances in our lives that necessitate changing our schedule. He prompts a stranger to call us about a project or work we never dreamed of and which opens up a whole new world for us. He causes things to happen which change the direction of our lives. Life becomes exciting, and we know it is God opening doors for us and allowing us to work with Him.

One of the problems we have in our new encounter with God is a feeling of unworthiness. Why should God be interested in me? After all, look at what I have done, and where I have been! I have fallen and failed so many times, and I never let God be a part of my past life. Why, now that I need Him, should He show any interest in me?

That, precisely, is the issue that baffles all of us. It has baffled every saint when they became involved with God. We all carry so much baggage with us when we arrive at God's doorstep. We cannot help but approach Him with bowed heads and humbled hearts. We have lived life to varying degrees of self-centeredness and have been badly mangled in the process. We are only too conscious that we have not had much time for God in the past, and have sinned, sometimes miserably. Why should God even care? If we treated a human this way, we could reasonably expect to be turned away. However, we are dealing here with a person who does not follow the ordinary pattern of human responses, and who does not nurse an offended ego. We are dealing with the One who created us and loves us with infinite tenderness, who looks upon our sins not as a moral theologian or a judge weighing the gravity of our guilt, but as a father or mother who cares, and who looks upon our sins as feeble attempts at learning how to live. We are like a child whose limbs are weak. The child tries to walk but falls, and keeps falling until she is strong enough to steady herself. It would be a cruel parent who would punish a child for falling when learning to walk.

That is the way it is with ourselves. God is very realistic. After all, He made us and knows quite well how we function. We may be shocked by what we see in ourselves but God understands the dynamics of all the complex needs and forces that rage within us. He understands only too well how blindly we are driven to find our place in life and to resolve the many conflicting cravings that stir within us. He would not be very realistic, if, after having made us this way, He would shun us for acting out the way we were programmed. And, indeed, He is not that way. Jesus tried all through His life to convince people of the deep understanding His Father has of human beings. The story of the prodigal son is a wonderful example of this. The story is really about the prodigal father when you analyze it. What father would treat such an irresponsible son the way that father did, giving him a share of the inheritance even before he died? Then, after the son leaves home and wastes his goods on pleasures, and has the nerve to come back to his father, the father runs out to meet him, dotes over him, throws a party for him, and does not even bring up the past. Jesus is obviously telling us something He wants us to understand about His Father. That is the way He is toward all of us. He gives to us lavishly. We are all prodigal children who have spent on ourselves most of what God has so generously given to us, then when we are hurting, we come back to Him with little left of all He gave us. That is the way we function. We do not know any differently. It is the rare person who is close to God from childhood. Most of us come back to God later in life, carrying with us terrible burdens of guilt and pain and anguish, after having wasted or hoarded most of what God has entrusted to us. God is always glad to see us coming back to Him from the distance, and He reaches out to greet us and welcome us.

We worry about things we have done, and the hurt we have caused. We worry about those we love and the pain they carry. God lifts that burden from our hearts and takes it to Himself, and assures us that He will heal those wounds and ease the pains we have caused and watch over those we love. That is the way God is. As time passes, we feel the suffering beginning to ease and our loved ones finding their way and in the process finding peace. The mistakes we made in the past are like footprints in the mud covered by the winter snow which in the springtime are revealed not as muddy footprints but as wildflowers all along the trail. He makes all things new. For God it is the present that is important. He heals the wounds of the past so they cannot destroy what we have newly found in His love for us.

As the presence of God becomes more pressing and more convincing, it is important that we do not distract ourselves from it. He is trying to befriend us. We should look upon this as a privilege and a gift, and treasure it. We do this by taking the time out of our busy schedules and going off by ourselves and spending some time with God. We do not have to pray verbally or feel that we have to talk to Him. Just being in His presence is all that is needed. He is the One who has things to say to us. It is for us only to listen. What we hear will not be words, but feelings of assurance, a sense that He is nearby, indeed, in our very souls. At times, the feeling of His presence will be overwhelming, and you will feel as if you are being lifted out of yourself, and that you could not possibly endure any more emotion without your heart bursting. Always remember that this is not a reward for being good. It is God telling you He loves you and is nearby. One day that will pass, and you may feel it is because you did something wrong or offended God. That is not the reason. That phase was only a passing experience God gave you to convince you He is real and that His love for you is real, and how ecstatic His love can be. It has little spiritual value otherwise. It is hard to grow when you are experiencing such sensible pleasures, as spiritual as they may seem to be. Their value lies in their ability to help focus your attention on God, and spend long periods of time centered on Him. In this way He can communicate with you and speak to your soul, gently altering your attitudes and your understanding, adjusting your way of viewing life and people and helping you gradually to see things the way He sees things. You will come through this phase a different person, more gentle and more understanding, and much more compassionate. Occasionally, however, some might develop a feeling of self-righteousness, thinking God is favoring them because they are so good, and then fall into the temptation of looking down on others for not having attained the spiritual heights they have reached. That can cause untold harm, not just to others but to ourselves as well. It can produce the kind of spiritual smugness that Jesus found so obnoxious in the scribes and Pharisees, who were so conscious of their perfection in keeping the law.

If we can avoid that pitfall we can greatly benefit from this phase of our spiritual journey. It is a powerful force in bonding us to God, and developing in us a strong sense of His continued presence within us, as well as a vivid awareness of His constant concern for us. Alongside of these tender expressions of God's love will be disturbing reminders of our human weakness. Just because we have these tender feelings does not mean we have all of a sudden become saints. Far from it. We are still what we always have been—frail, weak humans, prone to doing things that shame us. So, when we fall we should not be shocked, nor discouraged as if we have lost it all, or as if we have betrayed God. These falls, even though they be sins, still can be beneficial. They keep us aware of who we really are, and remind us that what we have been feeling for God is His gift and is not coming from our own inherent goodness. Our lapses into sin help to keep us humble in the realization that we have not progressed very far. Indeed, after a lifetime we still will not have progressed very far compared to the holiness of God we are trying to imitate. This whole spiritual world is indeed mystifying. This is one reason why it is essential we learn to turn over our spiritual lives to God. He knows where He wants to lead us and will do it gently and carefully so we will not be broken or get lost along the way.

V
~

NEW VISION

I AM AMAZED at the enthusiasm with which young people endure what for me would be grueling penance when they become interested in competitive sports. Athletes train for hours on end day after day to prepare themselves for competition. Musicians, also, practice for hours each day to keep in good form. And, particularly in our own day, just ordinary people perform grueling exercises to maintain good physical health.

The spiritual life is no different. We have to keep in shape. While I believe our spiritual lives should be marked by casual ordinariness, and not betray anything odd or outlandish, there are some things which are a natural part of spiritual development, and they are spiritual exercises. Spirituality is being in touch with our inner self, who we are, what we are, how we really think and feel, and how we relate to the world around us. Most importantly of all, how do all these things connect us with God who is the center of our lives. In the process of growing spiritually, what we are in essence doing is developing a comprehensive vision of life, a vision with God as the ever-present focus, giving clarity to what we see and feel, and meaning to our existence. Developing this vision is not easy. We can get lost. We can make mistakes which can be harmful. Witness the bizarre things people do in the name of religion. How often we see so-called religious people obsessed with religion and feeling they have to become the conscience for everyone around them, becoming nuisances by their incessant pressure on family and even strangers. How many people throughout history were burned at the stake and tortured in the name of religion? In our own day we see only too often the tragedies that take place because of religious fanatics. You can be sure each of those persons began their spiritual journey pretty much as everyone else, but because of some strange quirk took a wrong turn and ended up with ideas that are far from healthy.

To keep our minds healthy we have to be nourished on a healthy diet. And we also have to breathe. That is understood. Our nourishment comes from our reading, particularly the Scriptures; our breathing is our prayer life. Disciplining unruly desires is also essential. Reading opens our minds to the endless possibilities for spiritual growth, depending on where God is leading us and in what direction our energies drive us. We have to re-member everyone's spirituality is different. There is no monolithic spiritual model. Some may develop an inter-est in social justice. Others may be interested in the role of women in the world. Some may choose politics. Some may be concerned about the plight of starving people or the homeless. Some may be drawn to contemplation. Others may be content to just live ordinary lives within their limited circle of friends and neighbors. To a great extent it depends on where God is leading. Not that these interests are the whole of the spiritual life. They are not. They are the natural outlet, however, of our inner concerns which are an integral part of our spiritual lives, but they are not the essence of our spirituality. The essence of our spiritual lives is the partnership we have with God, the intimacy we have established with Him. Whatever He wants of us we are ready to accept. Wherever He leads we are prepared to follow.

Living this new life in the spirit is not easy. It is not natural for us, so we have to discipline our natural tendencies to adjust to this new and unfamiliar mode of behavior. Self-discipline is just as important for spiritual development as it is for physical and mental development. Just as athletes discipline themselves with endless calisthenics and motivate themselves by reading about their heroes, so spiritual athletes have to discipline unruly tendencies and regularly stimulate themselves to maintain their interest in spiritual development. If this regimen is lacking, interest will eventually wane, and they will drift back into their old ways. In the past, spiritually minded people read the lives of the saints. There was great benefit in that as well as enjoyment. It provided exciting and powerful ideals for people to ponder or imitate. In getting rid of saints, many modern Christians deprived themselves and their children of an army of inspiring witnesses to faith and heroic spirituality. I remember as a child I used to spend endless hours reading the lives of the saints, especially the early Christian martyrs. I was fascinated by their courage and their attachment to God. It was encouraging to witness the wonderful things God accomplished in the lives of these generous souls willing to sacrifice all to follow Him.

Young people today are rarely exposed to this literature. It is difficult for them to find much enjoyment in reading the Scriptures. The language and style is archaic. The stories are sketchy, and for most young people very boring. The lives of the saints were a big help in introducing young people to Christ. Lacking this there is a vacuum in which young people particularly either starve for ideals to imitate or create their own heroes, which, unfortunately, may be far from saintly. One of the saddest things in our society is that young people have no role models other than sports heroes. We have taken the saints out of their lives and now we pay the price. They have no Christian heroes to follow.

This developmental phase in our spiritual lives is critical. Critical, because at this point we are setting for ourselves the course for the future. Decisions we make now will affect the rest of our lives. The keystone of our new lives is freedom. Having found our Christ, our Savior, the first gift He gives us is our freedom. Freedom to be ourselves, freedom to follow Him, freedom to make our own choices. Unfortunately, many people do not feel comfortable with freedom. They must find for themselves a leader, a guru, or a mentor to take over the direction of their spiritual lives who will tell them what to do and how to think. A guide and counselor is understandable, as in sports or music or in any pursuit, but that is not enough. Many mistakenly believe they have to be led each step of the way.

I am presently reading a book about an organization within the Catholic Church that demands total obedience of its members. They must obtain permission from their leader for everything they do. He lays down for them guidelines even for their change of underwear. They are told they must break contact with their families and not share the work of their organization with any of their family members. When young people are recruited they are ordered not to tell their parents about their joining the society. Members are obligated to lay bare the state of their souls to their leader. Any new ideas about their spiritual lives they must share with their leader for his approval. He has total control over their souls. This has the ring of the diabolical about it. It is frightening.

Such behavior strangles the freedom Jesus won for us. It strips from people their dignity as children of God who should have direct access to their heavenly Father, and gives a human being veto power over the Holy Spirit's work in a person's life. It deprives them of the joy of being free to be themselves and enslaves them to their leader's wishes, no matter how apparently lofty their goals. Even God does not demand the kind of control over lives that this group demands of its members. Such unhealthy societies limit the redemption of Christ, and interfere with the Holy Spirit's work in the members' souls. The overall purpose of the group is to gain power in the Church and in society. To this end they befriend the wealthy, the well educated, and the powerful. The poor are not of great interest. The radical departure from the spirit of Jesus is clear, but to assure the maintaining of their goals, they must demand that their followers give up their freedom and follow their leader's wishes.

Freedom is essential in the spiritual life if we are to respond to the Holy Spirit, and grow in God's grace. We see this clearly in the lives of the Old Testament prophets. They had a most difficult role to play in God's plan. God had set up a teaching authority in Judaism from Moses through the high priests and the scribes and Pharisees. God guided the religious life of His people through them. The prophets were always vulnerable because in times of crises, when the religious leaders failed God, He would choose these men from outside the teaching authority to deliver messages to the people. This aroused the jealousy of the priests and the king that God should snub them and choose a nobody to provide guidance for the people. As a result, religious leaders persecuted and killed the prophets. So, it is easy to see why the young prophets panicked when God called them. Understandably they were reluctant to follow God's prodding because they knew full well what their fate would be. It was precisely these brave persons who are the heroes in the Bible, with many books of the Bible named after them. No one remembers the names of the scribes and Pharisees or what the priests did, other than that they killed the prophets. The prophets were special because they allowed themselves to be free to listen to God and respond to His call.

We see the same phenomenon today. Church leaders are stuck in sterile, worn-out forms and indulge in global politics and international financial dealings, which no doubt is in some way necessary. But God's people are starving with unfilled needs which grow ever more critical with each passing day. And little is done. So, we see God bypassing the teaching authority and speaking through ordinary people like Dorothy Day, or Cesar Chavez, or some of the more sensible and forward-looking theologians who prick the consciences of the shepherds so they will wake up and heed the needs of the flock. History again repeats itself. The prophets are punished or ostracized for listening to God and for delivering His messages to the people. In the past, God could use the prophets for His special work because they were free to listen to what He was telling them, and were not enamored with things of the past. They could have chosen not to listen. After all, who were they to tell those consecrated by God what they should teach or how they should act? But the true prophets chose to be open to God's call and to obey His instructions.

Prophets are only one example of people who listen to God. Each person has a mission just as important if not as dramatic as that of the prophets. We also must have the freedom to follow where God directs if we would accomplish the role He has designed for us.

Freedom, however, is not easy to handle. Some people panic at the thought of being free. A number of years ago I was chairman of a human rights commission and was also on an advisory board for the state office for the aging. Concerned about the elderly in the prisons who were no longer a threat to society, I set up a committee to work for their release from state prisons. At first, the prison officials could not locate most of the inmates targeted. They had become lost in a sea of paperwork and there was no record of their existence on the computers. When they finally found them, we were shocked to find that the inmates were happy enough remaining lost and did not want to be released. They had found security in their surroundings and were quite content to stay there until they died. They were afraid they could not handle living free outside. There are many people with that same fear of freedom. Whether it comes from insecurity or not wanting to take responsibility for their actions, the effect is the same. They are afraid that being free they might fail or be held accountable for decisions they might make. They would rather be told what to do and not have to make decisions. If someone has a problem like that, the spiritual life is difficult because a relationship with God involves making decisions, decisions to alter your understanding of things, to look at God in a different light, to follow where God may want to lead you. For persons like that it may be a help to have a spiritual director, not to have veto power over decisions but to be used as a sounding board for ideas, and as a help in resolving issues that may be complicated or confusing, and to offer suggestions for the person to consider. The director should be a person of faith who understands the spiritual life, is intelligent, and has common sense.

People do not always realize the joy of being free.

This is because many have a problem with how to use their freedom. It is the same problem children have. How often they complain, "Mother, I'm bored." Boredom will always be a problem unless we learn how to use our freedom. It can be a great help if we are good readers. There are volumes of solid spiritual writings for persons at all stages of the spiritual life, some boring, some not only helpful but exciting. We should acquaint ourselves with these books and schedule a few minutes from our busy schedule each day to enjoy them. They can open up for us vast horizons and present invigorating new challenges for us to consider.

Besides reading, prayer is essential. Our relationship with God grows from our constant awareness of His presence in our lives. At first it is difficult to think of Him. But as His presence becomes more real, our sense of His nearness blossoms into an intimate communing with Him in a beautiful kind of prayer. It may be a monologue, or it may be perceived as a kind of dialogue. In prayer God works on our attitudes. He alters our vision, our understanding of life. Over a period of time spent communing with God, we will notice our attitudes changing toward everything. We think differently about God. We think differently about material things. We think differently about ourselves and others. We think differently about rich people and poor people. We see God's creation and everything in it as sacred. Given the time God will eventually transform our whole life. He does this so subtly we do not even know it. Others see it and might on occasion make the remark,

"What a beautiful person you have become!" and the remarkable thing is that you do not even know what they are talking about, because God has accomplished this so quietly that you were totally unaware of what was happening. This is what St. Paul meant when he wrote, "I live, now not I, but Christ lives in me."

Placing ourselves at God's disposal may take a bold leap of trust, but it will probably be the most important decision of our lives. Disciplining ourselves and following our spiritual exercises will strengthen us in our new lives and light up the way on our new and bold journeys.

VI

IN DUE

SEASON

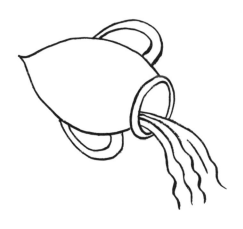

ONE OF THE first questions we face as we begin our new life with God is where to start. We understand that it is not anything we can do that will win us salvation. That is a free gift from Christ. But we instinctively know that we must contribute something of ourselves and prove our faith and love. St. Paul said we are "to work out our salvation in fear and trembling." Usually we decide that the best way of doing that is by keeping God's commandments. The temptation might be to start a ruthless self-analysis to ferret out all our sins and unruly desires, in a frantic effort to give up sin, even if we have not been terribly bad. In a short time we find ourselves fighting a thousand battles on a thousand different fronts. If we are particularly strong-willed we can be quite successful, but before long we find ourselves almost totally drained of energy, and when we fall, which we most certainly will, we can become so depressed we will be tempted to give up.

While it is important for us to try to do what is right and be virtuous, it is not possible to accomplish this overnight. Nothing in nature grows overnight. Plants start with a seed. The seed germinates, grows into a seedling, then a full-grown plant. Flowers appear, then fruit. All in good time, or, as Jesus put it, "in due season." Everything in nature grows the same way, slowly, step by step until it reaches maturity. The human person grows that way too. It takes years for our bodies to grow to maturity. It takes as many years for us to grow to intellectual maturity. The same is true for emotional and psychological maturity. That may take forty or fifty years. I remember an incident which took place at a party I attended. A lady was growing impatient with her husband and made the remark to him, "Harry, when are you going to grow up?" She was talking about emotional maturity. Harry was seventy-five years old. Emotional maturity sometimes takes a very long time. It is the way we are made. It has to be the same way with spiritual growth and maturity. We may think we can change overnight, but nature does not work that way. Spiritual growth is slow. It takes not just a few years, but a lifetime. We struggle to be good, to do the right thing, to make prudent decisions, to help others, to be faithful in prayer. Yet we still fall and fail, even with our best efforts. And after a lifetime of trying to discipline and perfect ourselves so we can be wise and strong and prudent and well disciplined, we get old and senile and start to lose it all. It is almost as if God is smiling at our efforts and does not take us quite as seriously as we take ourselves. And we wonder, maybe it is just our goodwill and our efforts God wants, as feeble as they may be. Perhaps He is not too terribly concerned about the measurable success we look for in trying to be holy. Maybe what is important to God is the unrelenting struggle on our part to do His will, to be sensitive to the pain and anguish of others, and our reaching out to help them. We have to understand this when we start so we do not become discouraged.

Concentrating on self-perfection and rooting out sin can become an almost total absorption, and can develop into a very self-centered spirituality. This was the spirituality of the scribes and Pharisees that Jesus criticized so vehemently, a spirituality that deteriorated into an obsessive pursuit of self-perfection, and self-adoration rather than a life of self-forgetting love that flowed spontaneously from a deep relationship with God. That is the kind of spirituality Jesus was trying to instill in people's hearts. And that is the path we should travel.

What is remarkable about Jesus' relationship to people we would call sinners is the relaxed and easy way he mingled with them. No one felt uncomfortable with Him. Nor should we feel uncomfortable in Jesus' presence, in God's presence. He does not want us to be uncomfortable with Him. The constant thrust of Jesus' message was to help people feel relaxed with His heavenly Father. "Why are you all so worried . . . Stop worrying, your heavenly Father will take care of you." The story of Jesus and the woman at the well points out graphically Jesus' attitude toward just ordinary people. Jesus chose to meet that woman on that particular day, knowing full well what she was. She was married five times and the fellow she was living with presently she had not married. Yet Jesus picked her to be the messenger, or the missionary to that Samaritan village. This Jesus who preached only the highest of ideals, including the highest ideals on marriage, this same Jesus could see goodness beneath the surface of that woman's life and pick her to be the missionary to her neighbors. God is not shocked or deterred by our weaknesses and our failures, as humiliating and shameful as they may be. He is concerned about the sincerity of our efforts and the intensity of our struggling to be good, and the goodness in our hearts. That is what is important to God. Life is so complicated, especially today, it is sometimes near impossible to live the ideals churches insist on and which we try so hard to follow. So many of us have had difficult lives in the past and it is not easy to erase the unwanted habits of a lifetime. They haunt us and with the best of efforts they are often too much for us, and we fall. It is often much harder for some people than for others. I know two boys. One finds it easy to be good and to be successful. The other seems to always make mistakes and out of poor judgment does things that are shocking. It seems that with the best of efforts he just does not know how to do things right. At the time he thinks what he did was right, but it ends up a mess. And the heartbreaking thing is, he tries so hard. I cannot help but think that that boy's struggling against such difficult odds endears him to God. He is the kind of person Jesus enjoyed associating with.

I also know a man in prison, a beautiful human being, who has a prayer life unmatched by anything I have come across in the outside world. The man is like Christ to the other inmates, but he knows he could never be trusted outside again because of his difficult and dangerously mixed-up personality. As with these people, it is not the tangible success that gives value to our lives, but the intensity of the struggle. Every single one of us is severely handicapped. God sees that. It is our handicaps that entitle us to God's mercy.

We have to get past a preoccupation with our sins. The thrust of our spiritual life should not be sin-oriented or Satan-oriented. It should be God-oriented. We should concentrate on developing a personal relationship with God, and through openness in our prayer lives, let God into our lives so He can guide us. As we get to know Him we cannot help but fall in love with Him. The intimacy and warmth of that relationship will deepen our insights and understanding and will help us outgrow our sinful tendencies, one by one. As an example, before we met God we may have been envious of the success and accomplishments of others, eating our hearts out because we could not have the same good fortune that they had. Now that we have met God and know how special we are to Him and that He has a very special work for us that nobody else can accomplish, our lives are given a meaning and a value that takes all the envy out of our hearts. We could not care less what someone else has. We now know we are special and are important to God. The same thing happens with our other vices. One by one we outgrow them, and in outgrowing them we get rid of them. That is a psychologically healthy way to attack our weaknesses and our limitations, by getting rid of the underlying problems which cause the sins.

I do not mean to give the impression that it is all right to sin. God forbid! What I am talking about is becoming so absorbed with ourselves and so determined to get rid of all our sins that we focus more on self than on God. We will become conscious when we are about to do something wrong, and we naturally should try to correct ourselves. Others are usually quite good at pointing out our limitations and faults. They are a big help. Our daily examination of conscience also goes a long way in helping us identify our mistakes. When we notice them we correct them, or at least try our best to correct them. We may not always succeed, especially if they are the expressions of deeply ingrained habits.

Our friendship with Jesus goes a long way in replacing our old ways of doing things with a multitude of nice things. These nice things fill up our lives as the not so nice things gradually fade from the pattern of our lives, and with these not so nice things are included our sins. The important thing about spiritual growth is that it should be psychologically healthy. It is a growth process and as much as we might like to become perfect, our progress has to follow a pattern that is not under our control.

To a great extent that pattern is determined by God. Since each of us is unique and has been created to do a special work, our life is a training process. God leads us through a set of experiences that prepares us for our particular work. If God calls a person to be a judge, He is not going to give that person a warm, affectionate nature and expose the person to a set of situations that will cultivate a sympathetic understanding of why problem people do the terrible things they do. It might be a nice trait to see in a judge, but if that trait predominates, the person would find it very difficult to sit in judgment.

If God calls a person to manifest His kindness and love to a hurting world, He is not going to give that person a personality that is rigid and insecure, and needs to see everything in sharp contrasts of black and white, good and evil, and judge people unfeelingly on harsh, rigid standards. He would give that person a kind personality, capable of seeing good in the most abject of human outcasts as He does, and filled with an infinite patience to reach out and pick up those who are beaten down so they can continue struggling on their way to God. The limitless variety of needs in humankind necessitates a limitless variety of functions for all of us to perform as we work together to help one another and bring out the beauty in His creation.

As a result the training process for each of us is different. No two persons will follow the same route in the spiritual life, and no two persons will be at the same place along the way. This is why it is so insensitive for us to pressure others to be the way we think they should be. It is none of our business. Each of us belongs to God, and God works mysteriously within us, slowly and patiently building up what He wants to accomplish in the unseeable recesses of our souls. Our good example and our kind words are prodding enough. People have to respond to God when they are ready, not from pressure by outside forces. In a rare case, perhaps, a weak person might need the discipline of a strong friend, but that cannot always be presumed.

Since God leads us each in our own way, our spiritual life will assume an aura totally different from that of everyone else. Each of us is one of a kind. Our spirituality then will be one of a kind. This is shown dramatically in various people's lives. I met a man at a wedding party one day. He was in a wheelchair and cornered me for the better part of an hour. He was badly deformed and had been that way from birth. We had a very pleasant conversation and when I learned he had a job I asked what kind of work he did. He told me he was an engineer and worked for the state. I was impressed. I guess he could see that I was impressed and went on to say, "I suppose some people would think that I should have been aborted, but I have had a terrific life, and I really love my work." This man's life is a living sermon. He does not have to say a word.

The story of Benedict Labre, who lived a couple of centuries ago in France, always impressed me. As a young boy he wanted to be a Trappist monk. He applied a number of times to the Order but each time was sent home. Finally, he realized God must have something else in store for him. He went home and told his parents he felt God was calling him to Rome. Reluctantly they let him go. In Rome he became a tramp, wandering the streets with other tramps. He dressed in rags and became widely known as one of the homeless who wandered the streets accepting scraps of food and clothes people would give to them. As time went on people began to realize there was something different about this tramp. One day some friends found him in a quiet glen on his knees absorbed in prayer. He stayed that way for the longest time. His companions were deeply impressed. They also found out that he had the rare gift of counseling people with the most complex problems and bringing them peace. His reputation spread throughout Rome and soon strangers from all walks of life came to talk to him; lawyers, doctors, judges, women in society, bishops, cardinals, as well as just ordinary folk. His wisdom and understanding enabled him to bring peace to the most troubled souls. When he died the church was packed with people. After his burial, people came from all over Europe to visit his grave and ask his intercession with God. The healings and graces people received were so overwhelming the Vatican was forced to start the process for his canonization as a saint, and in record time he was proclaimed a person of rare heroic holiness. On the day of the canonization Mass, in the crowded St. Peter's Basilica way up above the heads of all was the glorious painting of this sainted tramp dressed in his rags, held up for the veneration and admiration of all the faithful. What a strange vocation! And you cannot help but ask why. But it was at a time when the whole Christian world had become so materialistic that spiritual things meant little to people. So God called this young man to give up everything and wander the streets of Rome with other homeless people, dressed in the stinking rags of a tramp.

All the while God molded in the depths of his soul a holiness that transcended anything people had ever witnessed, and held up the remarkable spirituality of this lowly beggar for the admiration and example of all. It was no doubt a difficult vocation for one to follow, but St. Benedict was always a happy man, so he must have found a strange satisfaction in the realization he was following where God was leading him.

The life of St. Frances Cabrini is another remarkable story. As a young nun from Italy, her health was so poor no one thought she would live very long, and rather discounted her as far as being of much use to her Order. With her intense love of God and bold holiness, and her deep love for the poor, especially immigrants, she quietly and patiently founded over two hundred hospitals throughout the United States and Central and South America.

We never know how God is going to use us. What is important is that we remain open to Him and be ready for Him to use us in whatever way He sees fit. We can be sure we will never be disappointed. God will eventually turn our lives into an adventure that will bring a joy and satisfaction and a peace unlike anything we have ever known.

VII

ONLY

ONE THING

IS NECESSARY

WHEN YOU REALIZE the variety of functions God
has to invent to facilitate the complex influences we all
have on one another and understand the intimate part
He plays in each individual's life, you cannot help but
wonder at the mystery underlying the development of
spirituality. It is not as if God just supercharges individuals to keep His commandments thereby immediately
setting them on the fast track to heaven. Spirituality is
not that simple. Attaining heaven is not determined
merely by our keeping laws. Laws demand only the minimum in required behavior. Even though God gave us
the commandments and is concerned about our living
good moral lives, He is not obsessed with rigid obser-
vance of laws. That is why in the only example Jesus
gave of the Last Judgment, He said nothing about the
commandments, but spoke about our love for helping
people. "Come, blessed of my Father into the kingdom
prepared for you from the beginning of time, for when I
was hungry, you gave me food; when I was thirsty, you
gave me drink. When I was naked, you clothed me;
when I was sick, you cared for me. When I was in
prison, you came to visit me."

Spirituality is not developed in a vacuum. All of our
lives are intertwined and closely tied up with one an-

other. God does not create us to live in isolation. He created each of us incomplete, so we would need one another, so we could help one another, so we could reach out and touch one another's lives. Holiness is growth in godliness, and God is not self-centered. He is a giving God, always sharing the immensity of His infinite goodness with His creatures. Our holiness, then, is authentic when it is reaching out to others, sharing with others what God has poured so lavishly into our own lives. Though He works with each of us personally, molding in us His own inner life, He channels through ourselves and others what we all need for our survival and our growth, so we become the woof and warp of life's tapestry. The real work of our spiritual life lies essentially in what subconsciously takes place beneath the surface of our daily life, as God uses events and circumstances as well as people to alter our thought patterns, clarify our vision, reset the direction of our life, and realign our personality to harmonize with Jesus' own inner life.

Once we become aware of the complex way God works in our lives, it becomes clear why it is critical for us to be attuned to God's presence and sensitive to His voice. While it is impossible for us to be perpetually aware of His presence because our lives are so harried, we can still snatch brief moments of quiet time each day to listen to Him and become attuned to His unheard voice within us. It is at times like this, though not only at times like this, that we become aware of new insights into ourselves, our understanding of God, and the marvelous way He works throughout His creation. You may be sitting, thinking, someday, worried and concerned about the mistakes you made in the past, and all the sins of which you are now so ashamed. You feel humbled and unworthy of God, and wonder if He can ever really forgive you, even though you have long since repented of those sins. In the middle of your reveries, a calming thought crosses your consciousness, "Your sins, as humbling as they may be, are all forgiven. They are part of the past, and as such they no longer exist. You are now a new person, a new creation, washed clean and renewed in my Blood. You may still make mistakes. It is human. But I also see your love and I know the many good things you do for others in need. So, do not worry! Do not be afraid! You are a good person and I take delight in you. I love you and I am always by your side. So, do not be anxious, and do not be ashamed. I love you just as you are."

That insight, which is the way God communicates, while it may have taken only a fraction of a second, can affect your whole life, giving you, as it does, the key to finally loving yourself as you are, knowing that God loves you just as you are. You can see from this the simple but highly effective way God works within us as He shares with us His understanding and His insights. It is in this way that we grow. Over a period of time thousands of these insights replace our former way of thinking as we gradually grow to become almost a new person. This "magic" of God's saving and sanctifying grace is expressed in a touching way in the poem about the old violin.

The Touch of the Master's Hand

'Twas battered and scarred, and the auctioneer
Thought it scarcely worth his while
To waste much time on the old violin,
But held it up with a smile.
"What am I bidden, good folks," he cried,
"Who'll start the bidding for me?"
"A dollar, a dollar;" then, "Two! Only two?
Two dollars and who'll make it three?
Three dollars, once; three dollars, twice;
Going for three—" But no,
From the room, far back, a gray-haired man
Came forward and picked up the bow;
Then, wiping the dust from the old violin,
And tightening the loose strings,
He played a melody pure and sweet
As a caroling angel sings.

The music ceased, and the auctioneer,
With a voice that was quiet and low,
Said, "What am I bid for the old violin?"
And he held it up with the bow.
"A thousand dollars, and who'll make it two?
Two thousand! And who'll make it three?

Three thousand, once, three thousand twice,
And going, and gone," said he.
The people cheered, but some of them cried,
"We do not quite understand
What changed its worth." Swift came the reply:
"The touch of a master's hand."

And many a man with life out of tune,
And battered and scarred with sin,
Is auctioned cheap to the thoughtless crowd,
Much like the old violin.
A "mess of pottage," a glass of wine;
A game—and he travels on.
He is "going" once, and "going" twice,
He's "going" and almost "gone."
But the Master comes, and the foolish crowd
Never can quite understand
The worth of a soul and the change that's wrought
By the touch of the Master's hand.

We are all battered and beaten. We cannot go through life without being scarred. God knows that. He takes it for granted and goes on from there. That is why the story of the prostitute in Simon the Pharisee's house is so significant. The woman was far from being a pinnacle of virtue. The only thing that made her stand out was her brand of sin. Prostitution is not looked upon kindly by society. Jesus, however, could see past her sin and detect great goodness underneath her tattered reputation, and could praise her to the Pharisees at table.

There are sins a lot less honorable than prostitution, but we do not penalize their perpetrators. Take an upstanding judge who mercilessly sentences to ten or twenty years a poor black who cannot pull strings to plea bargain, when he would give perhaps only a suspended sentence to a middle-class white person with connections in the exact same circumstances. In the eyes of God that kind of sin is heinous compared to prostitution, but the judge will still be highly respected in the community, while the prostitute will be looked upon with contempt. The remarkable thing about God is that He will still take the judge as He is and see goodness in him as well, and will work to transform his life into something ultimately God-like.

The moving story of the eighteenth-century sea captain John Newton has touched everyone familiar with it. After leaving the Royal Navy in disgrace, he became involved in the slave trade, eventually acquiring his own ship. For years he transported slaves to the New World, living a life of debauchery. His life changed one day, though, when during a violent storm at sea he turned to God and begged Him to save his life and the lives of his crew. At the time he had been reading the *Imitation of Christ* by Thomas a Kempis, and this had brought back to Newton memories of his own pious mother, and strongly influenced his turning back to God. He later met John and Charles Wesley, who encouraged him to enter the ministry to which he was later ordained. He became best known for several hymns he wrote, one being perhaps the most famous hymn of all time,

"Amazing Grace." Like "Amazing Grace" itself, John Newton's life will always be a powerful testimony to the way God lifts us from the depths of our shame and awakens the goodness within us.

God's presence in the world makes itself felt in so many ways, particularly when people care for one another. The way in which the AA movement operates is a continuous manifestation of God's love weaving its way through the lives of people deeply beset by the most horrendous problems. This program always made me think that this is the way the Church should function. Members of the Twelve Step program develop an attachment to God that is touching in its humility and wonderfully childlike in its simplicity. It is big and grand enough to embrace people of all religions and races and every variety of pain and sin. It has the all-embracing goodness of God. Unlike churches which feel they must segregate people according to rigid doctrinal beliefs, and which crusade publicly for high moral righteousness in such a pompous way that sinners are frightened off, this program welcomes sinners and embraces them warmly. The sensitivity of people in the Twelve Step program is what genuinely religious people should be like in their caring for one another. No hour is too late, no time too long to help one who is on the verge of giving up or on the brink of despair. Their caring for one another is a touching manifestation of what Jesus meant when He said, "Love one another as I have loved you."

Every individual in this program could tell you of

the miracles of God's grace and the intimate way God has worked not only in their own lives, but in the lives of those they have sponsored or helped. And though they would not call themselves such, they are truly religious. It is clear when you become familiar with members of these programs how much they all depend on each other, and how deeply they have affected each other's lives. It makes God's presence in humanity so real and so tangible you feel as if you can almost touch Him. "Where there are two or three gathered together in my name, there I am in their midst." Where people touch one another so deeply and so palpably, you know that God is there. *"Ubi caritas et amor, Deus ibi est."* Where there is charity and love, there is God.

I recently received a letter from a person who belonged to AA. He said they used to meet in the basement beneath a church for their AA meetings. These meetings were tough meetings, dealing with everyone's pain and anguish, as well as their little victories and joys. It was the real world. Then when they went upstairs for church, they felt they were entering into a sterilized world where all those feelings and real-life experiences were out of place. The contrast was a jolt. Maybe we need both, but to those people it was more believable finding God downstairs than finding Him upstairs. That is sad, though perhaps we should join what happens downstairs to what takes place upstairs. Religion would certainly be more relevant to the hurting masses of humanity if people could express their hopes and dreams and pain and anguish to one another in the context of religious worship. As it is now our services are so antiseptic and sterile that people gathering for worship relate to others at only the most superficial level, and hardly ever get to know one another. It is a sad commentary on Christianity. Maybe that is one of the reasons why people feel religion is irrelevant, because they cannot find support and solace during times of crisis and pain. That is when real religion should be at its best.

The social aspect of spirituality begins to manifest itself early in our relationship with God. We can sense when He is using us to touch other people's lives. This became very obvious to me when *Joshua* first came out. I had known for quite a while God was pressing me to write. When I was doing nothing about it the pressure became greater and more insistent, until I decided that the only way I could write was if I resigned from the priesthood, which I was reluctant to do. One day my doctor called me into his office and told me I was fast heading for a stroke, and asked what I intended to do about it. Half in jest I said, "Suppose I retire and just write books?" He said it would be the best thing in the world for me, otherwise I probably would not be around by the end of the year. When I finally wrote the book and it began to circulate, letters poured in from people all over telling me how deeply the book touched their lives and brought them closer to God. I knew it had nothing to do with me, and I could see clearly that it was God at work through the book making people aware of His love for them. It was as if God chose to be powerless until someone allowed Him to work through

them, then wonderful things happened. This is a phenomenon in spirituality that may on the surface appear
to be merely a series of coincidences, but the persistence
and the timing is so obvious that after a while you know
it is God making Himself very much present in your life,
and serves to seal your bonding to God in a way nothing
else could.

VIII

TRANSFORMED

As our spirituality grows, our identification with Jesus grows, gradually assuming the character of His spirituality. Our understanding of God changes considerably. Previously our knowledge of God consisted of the remnants of ideas we carried with us from childhood. Our image of God to some extent was molded after our image of our earthly father, if we had any kind of healthy relationship with him. If we were close to our father, chances are we were also close to God. If we had an unhappy relationship with our father, it would have been difficult for us to have a good relationship with God especially if our parents were strong on religion and tried to force on us their image of God.

Now that we are close to Jesus, and we begin to see through His eyes, we also begin to absorb something of His understanding of His Father. We begin to see God as much bigger than someone human, or limited by characteristics of a particular sex. Jesus may call God His Father, but He describes His Father in ways that transcend anything merely paternal. God is too grand for that. The father in the story of the prodigal son was much more like a heartsick mother when confronted by the lost son returning home. He could not do enough to show the son he still loved him. Human love does not always go to the lengths of that father's love to welcome him back into the family. And it is precisely the impression Jesus wanted to give of His Father's love. It is compatible with the remark Jesus made about the Good Shepherd who goes about searching for the lost and the bruised and the hurting sheep. When He finds them He picks them up, places them on His shoulders, and carries them back home. "There is more rejoicing in heaven over one repentant sinner than over the ninety-nine just who have no need of repentance." Some may say that that is the Good Shepherd and Jesus is speaking of Himself. Think of other words of Jesus to Philip, "Do you not realize, Philip, that when you see me, you see the Father." The warmth, the tenderness, the all-encompassing concern of the Father for each of His children, aware even of the number of hairs on their head, shows a solicitude that far transcends anything merely human, paternal or maternal. He (for lack of an inclusive pronoun) transcends anything we could ever even comprehend. Jesus projects an image of His Father as always with Him, as the source of His strength, as the intimate partner in everything He does. He tells us that what His Father is to Him, He will be all these things to us as well if we open our hearts to Him. "To him or her who accepts me, my Father and I will come and make our abode with that person."

Jesus also tries to help us realize that His Father's concern is not just for humans, but for the least of His creatures. "Look at the birds of the air. They do not sow, nor reap, nor gather into barns. Your heavenly

Father takes care of them." We see God as a person with a love so immense and far-reaching in its comprehension that it extends even to the welfare of tiny creatures.

One of the most revealing traits about God that Jesus tried to portray was the idea of forgiveness. That was a revolutionary concept for people of Jesus' day, as well as for people of our own day. Though many of the prophets tried to project an image of God as extremely tender and doting over His beloved bride, Israel, Old Testament passages overwhelmingly portrayed God as an avenging God who thought nothing of instantly slaying thousands of His own people when they crossed Him. That was not how Jesus saw His Father. He tries relentlessly to show us that His Father is a loving, forgiving God. Jesus says to His followers that they should love their enemies and do good to those who hate them, and pray for those who persecute and calumniate them, so they might be children of their Father in heaven, who shows kindness to the just and the unjust. He then tells them to be perfect as their heavenly Father is perfect. The perfection He is referring to here is not perfection in the keeping of laws, but to what is mentioned just before, perfection in expressing genuine love even of your enemies. God's perfection is not about the keeping of commandments, it is about the expression of His ineffable love. Love is the definition of God. It is His essence. It is what makes God God. So, in enjoining us to be perfect like His Father, Jesus is challenging us to love as completely and as unselfishly as His Father, particularly with the unrelenting forgiveness of His Father's love.

Jesus is careful, however, not to portray His Father as a sentimentalist who condones lax and characterless moral behavior. "Not everyone who says to me, 'Lord, Lord,' will enter the kingdom of heaven, but those who do the will of my Father in heaven shall enter the kingdom of heaven. Many will say to me in that day, 'Lord, Lord, did we not prophesy in your name, and cast out devils in your name, and work many miracles in your name?' And then I will declare to them, 'I never knew you. Depart from me, you workers of iniquity.' " It is Jesus who metes out His Father's justice.

The warning to the unforgiving servant likewise conveys a balancing image of the Father. "And his master, being angry, handed him over to the torturers until he should pay all that was due him. So also will my heavenly Father do with you, if you do not forgive your brothers from your hearts."

This idea of forgiveness is clearly an essential element of Jesus' spirituality. Spirituality is modeled on God's life, on God's essence. Forgiveness of others' injuries stamps our spirituality as genuine and authentic. Not to be forgiving reduces our spirituality to a merely human imitation of the real thing, and yet forgiveness is not something that has taken hold among Christians. Perhaps the reason is because we cannot understand the logic behind Jesus' insistence on forgiveness. On the surface Jesus seems to be placing a burden on people, which was not like Him. Ordinarily, He tries to lift burdens from people's hearts and to lighten their already heavy burdens. This responsibility of forgiveness seems gigantic and indeed almost psychologically impossible. Peter, after obviously struggling with this issue for some time, approached Jesus one day and, with a certain feeling of pride, said to Him, "Lord, how often shall my brother sin against me, and I forgive him? Up to seven times?" Jesus' answer was a complete shock. "I do not say to you seven times, but seventy times seven times."

What is Jesus driving at? How can any of us forgive endlessly? This whole thing seems contrary to everything Jesus has come to stand for. He is forever trying to make people's lives simple and more reasonable. Then, one day it dawned on me what Jesus was trying to accomplish. He had made the remark on one occasion that the law was made for man and not man for the law, then went on to justify something shocking which David had done because there was a human need. Jesus' concept of law had to do with what was good for people.

Applying that principle to forgiveness, it changes the whole context of Jesus' injunction to forgive. Scanning Jesus' own life for examples of forgiveness, I could not help but be amazed at all the insults and daily slights that Jesus encountered. And you never see Him taking offense. "Father, forgive them, they know not what they do" seems to be the overriding attitude in Jesus' mind, so he overlooks the hatred and plotting of the Pharisees, the ingratitude of the populace that received the constant benefit of His healing grace and walked away without a word of thanks, the rudeness of the apostles, the ignorance of the religious leaders who should have been His staunchest advocates, but turned out to be his bitterest enemies. Everywhere He manifests kindness and grace to all regardless of how they treat Him, which shows that Jesus practiced in His own life what He enjoined on His followers. It also became very clear then that Jesus did not intend to create an added burden for His followers. In fact, He was really giving them the key to inner peace, the key to His own transcending serenity. "Do not allow yourself to take offense when someone inflicts injury upon you. Understand the anguish and the pressures in their life and the pain that prompted their thoughtless or warped behavior, then you will pity them and keep at bay the pain and grief you would have suffered had you allowed the offense to take hold of you. In this way you will stay free and uncluttered with anger and resentment. I tell you this as the key to true inner peace." The fact that Jesus said, "Seventy times seven times" now makes sense. If you are going to forgive, you must forgive all the time, not just some of the time, otherwise it will not work. You can *never* let injury enter your soul if you want to maintain your tranquillity. Granted this may be difficult for the novice, but in time overlooking hurt can become second nature. A person's whole life can be transformed by this, the most divine of virtues.

Once Jesus establishes His place in our souls, the first gift He shares is peace. That is why forgiveness is important to Him, it preserves our peace. Inner peace is the fertile soil in which our spiritual garden can grow. Where there is turmoil it is almost impossible to develop an inner life. There is just no room for the thought or reflection which is essential for the development of a spiritual life. Jesus talks to us in the peacefulness of our souls.

Once serenity is established then God begins His work in earnest. We saw before how detached Jesus was from material things. He enjoyed what He saw in nature, in His Father's creation, and we find Him at times just sitting and admiring the beauty of the sea and the changing colors in the sky, the flowers in the field, the animals in nature. It may seem like a small thing, but just for the Gospel writers to mention it shows it impressed them and was significant. Many people pass through these things each day of their lives on their way to work, or driving in the country, and never notice the birds, or the clouds floating across the sky, or the flowers by the roadside. They are too preoccupied with business matters or with personal problems to notice anything outside themselves. They travel through life as if it were a dark tunnel. That is unfortunate. Seeing Jesus notice things in the world around Him shows the appreciation He had for what He found in nature, and the simple pleasure He derived from it. His delight, however, was always a detached enjoyment, which did not demand possession of what He saw as a necessity for His happiness. One of the problems we have is that we cannot just be content to admire and enjoy, we have to possess and feel we own what we see. That can become for so many of us an addiction which adds a complication to our life and takes away our peace of mind. Craving things becomes after a while a serious distraction and an obsession. Jesus speaks about this when He talks about it being more difficult for a rich man to get to heaven than for a camel to walk through the eye of a needle. Not that He was condemning the possession of things, but the distraction and the craving for them which simulates the worship and attention we should reserve only for God. If we are not careful, craving material things can take the place of our worship of God and cause us to do things that are evil and vile in order to maintain and increase our possessions, even destroying other people in the process. So, detachment from material possessions was a high priority in Jesus' approach to spirituality, and He exemplified this in His own life. He practiced a remarkable detachment from things. There is no record of His ever owning anything, even a coin or a trinket, though we see Him noticing and enjoying even the simplest things in creation. It is this detached delight in things that is His trademark and could serve us well as we try to develop a spirituality after His example.

Following Jesus' footsteps through the Gospels you notice His relationships with people. They are relaxed, casual. He is at home with high public officials, with lepers roaming the countryside, and with little children jumping all over Him, and the charm of it was that it was natural and not contrived. He did not go out of His way to make a thing out of being nice to a leper because this person was a leper. He embraced a leper just as naturally as He embraced an official from Herod's palace. That ability flows from His profound realization that each of us is a child in His Father's family, and each has equal dignity. We preach it, but Jesus believed it and we see in Him the form such belief takes in real life. It is stunning. It is magic in its effect on people.

Practicing this as an expression of our own spirituality is not easy and cannot be forced. As our faith deepens and as the Spirit quickens our awareness of the dignity of each child of God, grace must prompt our charity to reach out to everyone, so that no one will ever be to us a stranger. We cannot practice this beyond the faith and charity God gives us at any particular time. If we do not have it, we have to accept that fact temporarily and pray that God will one day give us the grace to practice that high degree of charity we would like to have. Charity cannot be forced. It must flow freely from the wellsprings of our own love. Practicing love of neighbor to this heroic degree is not easy and has its dangers and we have to be prudent. In this, particularly, we must have the simplicity of the dove but also the wariness of the fox as Jesus warned. Jesus could see through people and understand them at a glance. We do not have that ability, so we cannot operate as freely as Jesus. Even He was discreet, like the time He was headed for Jerusalem and decided not to go openly, because He did not wish to trust Himself to the crowd because He knew what was in their hearts.

There is another aspect of Jesus' life which is an

essential facet of His spirituality. That is the realization that He is here to do His Father's will. That should not be unique to Him. It should be the hallmark of each of us. We should all be here to do our Father's will. Jesus lived it. In following His way, this commitment should be a characteristic of our spirituality. This commitment flows from the realization that we were made by God for Himself, to fulfill a task He appointed for us. We belong to God, and when we rest our heads on our pillows at night, it should be with the comforting thought, "God, I finished my job for you today. I may not have done a perfect job, Lord, but I tried. My life is to do your work, Lord. I am yours. Keep me in your love. Keep my soul at peace."

Keeping ourselves aware that we are partners with God, and with Jesus, has an important effect on us. We know we belong to God, and He has to take care of us because we are doing His work. That gives us a feeling of security and a trust that no matter what may come up during the day, God will resolve the problems and bring about a happy conclusion.

A graphic story comes to mind from my childhood. During the Second World War, my father was drafted into the army. There were nine children at home at the time. Reporters came to the house for interviews. They asked my father if he was angry for being drafted, since he had an army of his own to care for. "No," he said. "There are times when we must fulfill our duty to our country." "But who will take care of your wife and all your children?" one of the reporters asked. To which my father replied, "If God can use me to take care of them, He can do just as good a job without me."

We have to have that tough realization that God is very much an active partner in our lives and He is determined to see our work through to completion. Jesus never had any doubt that His Father's work would be accomplished in His life. We must have that same assurance that God's work will be carried out in our lives as well. That is His will and He will not be frustrated. So, we have the assurance He will always be by our side with His guidance and His help, inevitably bringing to completion the masterpiece He has planned from all eternity for our lives. Things may go wrong occasionally, maybe even frequently. Problems may crop up, maybe even frequently. Health may crumble. Troubles may beset us on every side. Friends may leave us. Doubts may disturb us. Darkness may overwhelm us. Evil may haunt us. But that is all right. God will still be there by our side, making sure of our ultimate success. I have seen how tangible is the devil's anger when we do God's work. After traveling two hundred fifty miles to give a talk one day, then to be stuck in a traffic jam on the mountain highway within sight of the building where I had to speak, and then to get there just in time, though I missed a wonderful dinner, was too graphic to be a coincidence. On another occasion, to have an airline declare bankruptcy a half hour before my plane from Louisiana was to leave on a flight to a Southern Baptist University was too carefully calculated to have been an accident. Plus a host of similar occurrences that ultimately turned out all right. What a consoling thought this can be for us, knowing that God is with us to assure the completion of our work! I have seen it so often in my own life, and it never ceases to amaze me how persistent God is in bringing our appointed tasks to their fulfillment. It can give us tremendous stability and a remarkable feeling of confidence knowing that we are doing God's work, and that He is also our partner, and no matter how complicated or devious the route, we will ultimately be successful.

IX

FROM EARTH

TO GLORY

AN INTEGRAL PART of our spirituality is carrying the cross with Christ. This may seem morbid, but it really is nothing more than what is expected in any human love affair. If you deeply love someone you are willing to endure almost any pain or go to almost any lengths to prove that love. With God it is no different. Jesus said, "If you are not willing to take up your cross and follow me, you are not worthy of me." The cross or sacrifice will always be part of our life with Jesus, like pain is always a facet of true love.

Most pain, however, is not caused by our relationship with God. Frequently, our troubles are of our own making, or are just part of ordinary living. The pain of loss, the pain of illness, the pain of depression, the emotional pain that comes from so many unfilled needs, the pain of worry about loved ones, particularly children and their troubles, these kinds of pains are not due to commitment to God, but are just part of life. The comforting phenomenon, however, is the fact that they can all be incorporated into our life with God and can facilitate an even greater intimacy with Jesus, because it allows us to share with Him all these hurts and anxieties, and find in His friendship the comfort and guidance we need. Knowing how real is our friendship with

Jesus and how much we can trust Him to be a friend and help those we love when they are hurting, this adds a wonderful dimension to our spiritual life. God has the thoughtful knack of taking upon Himself our concerns about loved ones and our own troubles and helping us benefit from them in such a way that they become part of our training for work He is preparing for us later on down the road. Nothing that happens in our lives is wasted energy. God in some way will find a way to put it to good use sometime, somewhere.

I used to feel so sorry for my mother's best friend, Anna, who had what I thought was a most miserable life. As a young girl she had rheumatoid arthritis, which crippled her to the point where the doctors had to break both her legs to straighten them out. Besides this, Anna had a very painful and extreme case of psoriasis. Her whole body would become covered with scales from the painful illness. In spite of these problems she married. Within the year, she and her husband moved to California where he worked. Eventually Anna had a child. Soon afterward, however, her husband left her, far away from home and far from any possible help from family and friends. Throughout all this, though, she and my mother always corresponded, for thirty-five years.

One summer I decided to take my mother to California to visit her friend, whom she had not seen in all that time. When we tracked down the nursing home where Anna lived, and entered the ward and saw her, you could see she was crucified to a bed of pain. Her whole body was twisted from arthritis in every joint.

Anna immediately recognized my mother and myself and called our names. My mother started to cry. "Margaret," Anna said, "I hope you are not crying for me. I have to be the happiest person on this earth. If you only knew how close God is to me all the time. I don't think I could be happier." She had not been able to move her body for almost seven years, and was totally dependent on the staff to care for her slightest needs. Still, she had found profound happiness. I learned a lot that day, about God, about spirituality, about suffering, about so many things. It would take me a volume to unravel all the lessons of those few minutes of viewing a saint lying on a bed of pain. St. Paul once made the cryptic remark, "We must fill up in our own bodies the sufferings that are lacking in Christ." I could not fully understand how Jesus' sufferings were not enough. I understood that day what St. Paul meant. There are some privileged souls called by God to share in Jesus' sufferings and help Him in His redemptive work of saving souls who wander from God's grace. That is a type of cross that is very much a part of some people's following of Jesus.

There are also everyday crosses involved in following a spiritual life. The denial of things we enjoy is necessary because we must discipline our senses so we can become more attuned to spiritual things; that is a sacrifice and a little cross. The things God asks of us as we follow Him through our lives each day, like putting ourselves out to help one in need, or giving financial help to people in difficult straits, or making decisions to do the right and honorable thing when we could benefit greatly from doing something shady or downright dishonest. They are crosses directly involved in being faithful to Jesus. The training process God puts us through as He helps to toughen us up for solid spiritual growth, this can sometimes be painful. When you read the lives of the saints, there is hardly one who did not suffer intensely in his or her life. Suffering seems to be the crucible in which God burns out of our souls all that is petty and mean and gross and gradually molds us into something that resembles the divine. If God is going to make this lowly clay of which we are made into something divine, that process cannot be anything but painful. I like to think of a piece of coal and a diamond in this regard. Both are made of carbon. One is worthless, the other is priceless, even though they are both made of the same material. The difference is that a diamond is a piece of coal that has been subjected to the intense heat and pressures of the earth until all the impurities have been driven out of it. It then becomes a diamond, and priceless. You might say a diamond is a piece of coal that has suffered.

It is the same with ourselves. The purpose of our lives is to grow into a fully matured child of God, which means developing the life of God within us. Becoming spiritually mature means to practice the various virtues to an heroic degree. This can take place only if we encounter endless occasions to exercise these virtues. Take patience. How could we attain heroic patience unless we are subjected to many trying situations where we have to practice endless patience? Over time we attain a very high degree of patience. Or take the virtue of courage. How could we ever attain heroic courage unless we are put into circumstances that demand extraordinary valor and courage? Or heroic love. To arrive at a state of heroic charity, God must place us in the right and difficult circumstances and give us the grace to accomplish things that demand extraordinary love of God and of others. Gradually, our love will grow to a level we never would have thought attainable, and the wonderful thing about this growth in holiness is that it is mostly the work of God within us and is all so beautifully unself-conscious.

To all this growth you can see there has to be pain attached. It is almost impossible to grow spiritually without undergoing great sacrifice and enduring much pain, which Jesus called the cross. As my father used to say so frequently, "You can't raise children on sympathy." God is that way, and He realizes only too well that if He is to fashion us into something worthwhile, He will have to put us through strenuous exercises. Those exercises must of necessity be painful, just like athletes with their calisthenics and physical exercises. However, at the end of it we realize how worthwhile it all was.

One of the side effects of the purifying process God puts us through is a mellowing of our personality. When we first enter the spiritual life we tend to be rigid and exact in everything we do, and to be unreasonably demanding not only of ourselves but of others, not understanding why they cannot have the same enthusiasm about spiritual things that we have. After enduring the dark nights with the humbling experiences that are so much a part of that trial, we emerge very much changed in our attitudes toward ourselves and toward others. During that period of trial and suffering we learned in a tangible way the frailty of our own natures, and how dependent we are upon God just to maintain our spiritual equilibrium and avoid serious moral pitfalls. Experiencing our weaknesses without God's special help, we come through, chastened and meek, with a new appreciation of other people's struggles and weaknesses. This gives us a tolerance and an understanding we did not have before, and deepens our compassion for the pain and anguish others are going through on their way to God. This is particularly true if during our dark nights God allowed us to fall and experience the depths to which we can tumble without His special grace and support. We are no longer self-righteous in the harshness of our judgment of others and we can easily accept others where they are at. Not that we become indifferent to evil when we see it. But we are no longer judgmental and the approach we use in bringing Christ to others is with a gentleness and a humility that opens hearts more easily because they sense that our concern is genuine and that we are not about to mount a spiritual assault upon them from the ivory tower of our self-righteousness.

Having come through this most difficult phase of the spiritual journey, humbled and chastened, we are much more relaxed with ourselves and with others. We feel free to be casual and spontaneous in our relationships and are much less prone to pressure others to be what we think they should be. We can again begin to enjoy others and even find humor in their foibles and imperfections. Others begin to relax with us and can again enjoy our companionship, which is one of the remarkable traits that we have seen in the life of Jesus. He was always so relaxed with everyone. He moved so freely and so spontaneously through people's lives. People consequently always seemed relaxed and comfortable in His presence, even though they may have been sinners. They never sensed a critical spirit in Jesus. They seemed to sense He knew them, everything about them, and that He understood. It was not that He condoned their sins, but He had the understanding to realize that people grow at God's good pleasure and when God decides to give them the grace. People sensed this and felt comfortable enough to be themselves and enjoy being with Him. Contact with Him inevitably brought about profound transformation in their lives, but it happened slowly, naturally, and as God gave the grace. That is the way spiritual growth should be, not the result of neurotic pressure either from ourselves or from others.

Even though the cross is essential to the development of true spirituality, it does not hang over the life of Jesus and should never cast a pall over the life of His followers. Joy will always be the predominant spirit of Jesus' approach to our life with God. Jesus was above all else a happy person, and a person remarkably free, free from the grip of material things, free from unhealthy attachments to people, free from obsessive hang-ups and neurotic needs. It is a pleasure to watch Him move so easily through life, even with His knowing the troubles that were always impending. He never allowed Himself to be obsessed with worry or with a sense of doom. Problems He handed over to His Father, as if that was His business. He just did what He knew He had to do each day. In living this way He was able to manifest a remarkable detachment and continually radiate a spirit of joy.

This close relationship of Jesus with His Father and with the Holy Spirit is a unique phenomenon in religion. It manifests the inner nature of God as a family of persons, with diverse attributes but inseparably one. You can see the strength this gave to Jesus in His human circumstances, and in His own personal humanness. Jesus tried to share this with His followers, by introducing them to His Father, and later when they had grown mature enough to accept the Holy Spirit.

Community was important to Jesus. He did not work alone. He traveled in community. There was always a group who followed Him from village to village, consisting of His mother, his faithful relatives, and loyal women disciples such as Mary Magdalen, Salome, the wife of Herod's chief steward. His relationship with the apostles was community, each apparently with their own work to do. Judas carried the common purse and paid the bills and doled out alms to the poor. They slept around campfires at night when they were on their missionary journeys.

A separate community of the seventy-two disciples was set up to spearhead Jesus' arrival in various villages and towns. They had to be trained to do their work and also work in tandem with the apostles whose function was to be Jesus' *alter egos* in preaching the Good News and in carrying out His healing ministry. Not everyone was empowered to do that. From all this you get a clear sense that Jesus did establish a well-organized community, each with their own work and each expected to be responsive to one another's needs, and to be sensitive to each other's problems and aspirations as they grew closer and closer as a family. This idea of family was a trademark of Jesus' approach to religion, which immediately set His followers apart from the frigid legalism of the religion that had dominated their lives from the cradle to the grave. Jesus' idea of religion as family was not intended to be new type of legal structure, but a community of individuals who enjoyed their newfound freedom as God's children, allowed to be themselves. These community members could accept one another as they found each other without an obsession with placing people into legal religious straitjackets and forcing them into new molds. The purpose of community and family was not to dominate the individual but to be there for companionship, for support, for affirmation of one another's efforts, and to work together in spreading the wonderful joy and freedom they had found in Jesus, and to reach out to bring comfort, support, and healing to those around them in need. It was not long before they got the reputation for their outstanding love for one another. "See how these Christians love one another!" a prominent Roman was later to remark.

Jesus did have little rituals, as vehicles to share His own inner life, and to deepen His followers' oneness with Himself. These were simple rites, such as Baptism which could be performed at a pond or a running brook, if available, or if not by just simply pouring water. The Breaking of Bread, the sharing of Jesus' flesh and blood, so precious to the earliest Christians, could be performed around the kitchen table. Reconciliation could be accomplished as you walked along a roadside or a city street, or with an expression of remorse at the family gathering of the community, over a disloyalty to God or a scandal that brought shame on the community. Through the Laying on of Hands the apostles passed on to others the power and authority they received from Jesus.

This whole approach to religion and the type of spirituality it gave rise to was new in religious history and served to reunite the human family to its Creator and at the same time allowed people to enjoy the freedom of being newly adopted children of God, through a real infusion of God's life into their souls. The structure of religion then was to be in a subservient role in which religious leaders were to encourage, guide, teach, affirm, and help God's children to understand how their Father and the Holy Spirit were working in their lives and in the life of the community, and what was expected of them as loyal children of God and followers of Jesus.

The ultimate end of all this work and the spirituality

it generates is preparation for entrance into God's presence at the end of our journey through life. Heaven was the crowning glory of the life Jesus promised His followers. If Jesus taught nothing else, this teaching alone was enough to change the whole destiny of the human race. He was the first and only religious leader to speak authoritatively about the existence of heaven, a place He knew of because He came from there. "The eye has not seen, nor has the ear heard, nor has it ever entered into the imagination of man the wonderful things my Father has prepared for those who love Him." And on another occasion, "I go to prepare a place for you, and I will come back and take you along with me, so you can be where I am."

The development of spirituality, the growth of our life in God, flows naturally into a life with God after death, the kind of life in which we will see God and know Him in the same way He knows and loves us, a life in which we share with Jesus the eternal ecstasy of God's presence and the joyful and endless companionship of God's family and our own loved ones whom God has called home.